MOUNTAIN
SOLITUDES

Solo journeys in the Southern Alps of New Zealand

MOUNTAIN SOLITUDES

Solo journeys in the Southern Alps of New Zealand

Aat Vervoorn

CRAIG
POTTON
PUBLISHING

© Aat Vervoorn

Published by Craig Potton Publishing
98 Vickerman Street, PO Box 555, Nelson, New Zealand
© 2000 Craig Potton Publishing

Cover design: Robbie Burton
Editing: James Brown
Printed by Spectrum Print, Christchurch

ISBN 0–908802–64–1

CONTENTS

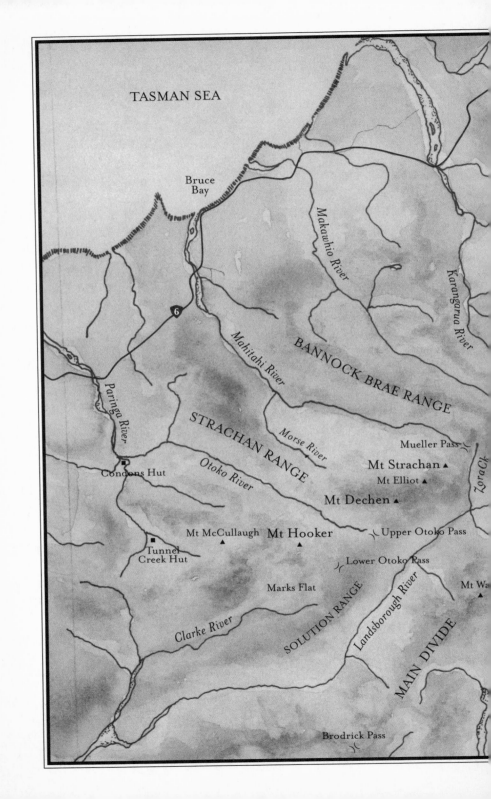

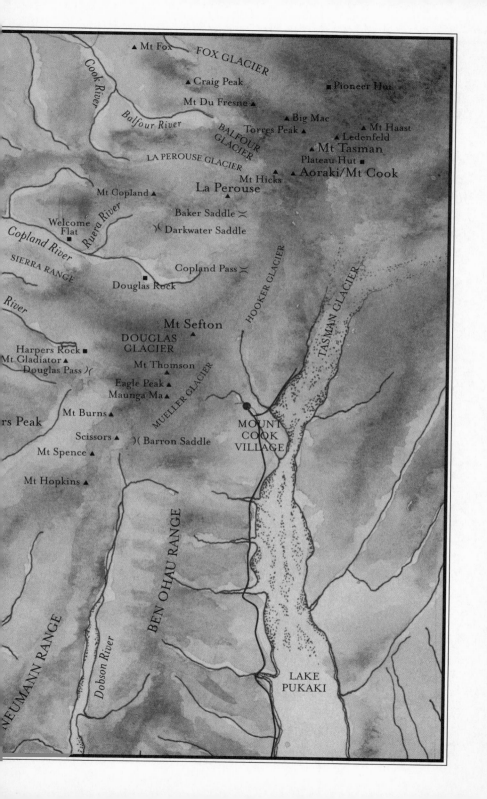

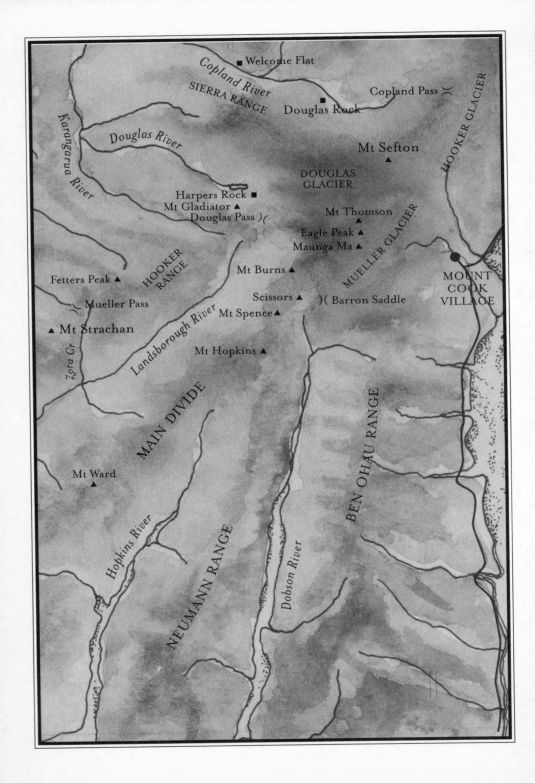

CHAPTER ONE

Adventure is a sign of incompetence.
— Vilhjalmur Stefansson

It was not because I wanted to that I headed for the Landsborough River. Eagle Peak made me do it.

I had come from Mt Cook Village, up the moraine–covered ice of the Mueller Glacier to climb the eastern face of Eagle Peak. At the toe of the Ngakanoi Glacier, where its meltwater thunders over ice–carved cliffs to the valley floor below, there are rock ledges; not sheltered, but big enough for a comfortable snooze on a clear night, and my night had almost been that. Dawn lit up the high glaciers of Mt Sefton, yet valley cloud was already forming as I started up the rock face directly above my camp.

At first the rock was loose and broken. Despite having left sleeping bag, stove and spare food on my ledge, and therefore carrying little except the rope, I felt uneasy as I climbed. Soon the rock became steep, solid, smooth. I moved up a vertical wall on small holds, then reversed down it, awkwardly, when the holds above began to look smaller still and I became afraid that retreating from higher up might prove impossible. I uncoiled the rope, fastened one end around me, took out the few bits of rock–climbing hardware I had with me, and set off again, trailing the rope behind me in case I needed it in a hurry, this time following an easier route up the wall.

With my attention focused on finding a way up the rock, I had not noticed cloud banks darkening the sky above and below me. There was no wind and the air was warm, close; sweat was running off me. After 500 metres of climbing, the top of the rock wall led onto a steep rib of snow. Here I became anxious, for the snow was wet and unstable. On both sides of the rib it was starting to slide as heavy shapeless masses fell off the warm rocks above, triggering movement. It was only a few days since the snow had fallen in a fierce southerly storm which had whitened the foothills and coastal ranges. Although it was steep, at least the rib I was ascending kept me out of reach of the avalanches that now began to sweep down the gully on my left, then curve out from the rock face below and crash with a roar on the slope of the Ngakanoi Glacier, not far from the ledge which yesterday evening had seemed a safe place to sleep.

Eleven years previously, when climbing neighbouring Mt Thomson, I had looked across at the route I was now attempting. I had told myself it would not be something to try were the snow new or soft; should the snow begin to avalanche on the steep upper slopes there would be no well-defined crests on which to keep out of harm's way. Now that observation seemed most astute and I was regretting not heeding my own counsel. Not far above me, the rib I was on merged into a broad snow slope, below a shallow gully that led up through a rock step to the upper slopes now heavily covered with new snow. From there a final rib of rock promised secure going to the summit. Once off the snow I would be out of danger.

It was necessary to move quickly, but my dash for safety was a slow-motion affair. Tiredness, nervous tension, the angle of the slope, and the knowledge that the Mueller Glacier was now more than a kilometre vertically below, all prevented my body from moving with the speed my mind knew was needed. I had moved out of the top of the gully, and was veering left to get out of the danger zone, when I heard the hiss of a wet snow avalanche above me. It bore straight down on me: not big, not fast, just frightening. I rammed my ice-axe into the slope, cowering behind the four or five centimetres of shelter its shaft provided, with head and arms pushed into the snow, legs braced. The snow cascaded over me, gathering volume and speed as it entered the gully, to sweep the slope I had just ascended and boom over the drop below. It was still reverberating from the valley walls when a second, smaller, avalanche followed the first. It gave me only a half-hearted shove as it passed, yet my shaking legs barely managed to withstand its force. A third would easily have swept me off the mountainside, like an insect blown onto a glacier by the wind. Soaked outside, dry from fear inside and trembling violently, I panted up to the final rib of rock, following the avalanche track now cleared of soft snow.

As I climbed the rocks towards the summit, I began to sense a presence, something external that was accompanying me and communicating wordlessly. It soothed and supported me; it sought to calm me, to help me regain control over myself and the situation. There was no illusion of a physical companion or the presence of an identifiable individual, neverthe-less I had a clear sense that this was a consciousness separate from my own, something independent of me that came unbidden, whose calming, reassuring effect was direct and immediate. The precise moment it came I cannot remember, nor the time when it finally left, but the experience continued for a long time. It was not overpowering or consuming, nor did it appear strange or mysterious. I felt no inclination to speculate whether it was a deity or some other visitor from a spiritual realm; I was simply glad that it was there and grateful for its influence. It remained near the edge of consciousness, quietly, discreetly, yet potent and undeniable.

On the summit of Eagle Peak it was winter. A freezing wind blew from the west, sheathing the rock of the Main Divide thickly in ice and blasting it with powdery snow that spun about me. For a moment, to my right, the top of Mt Thomson emerged from the cloud, high and snowy, then was gone again, leaving only rushing air, mist and cold.

I turned away from where Mt Thomson had disappeared and set off slowly along the crest of Eagle Peak in the direction of Maunga Ma. It was only a kilometre away, and from its summit a short steep ridge of snow led down to the beginning of the Ngakanoi Glacier; down this, all going well, I would able to return to my bivouac site and head for home. It was a sensible plan, but unfortunately not easy to carry out in the prevailing conditions. Despite the best efforts of the comforting presence, I was still shivering from nervous tension. To climb down the ice–coated rocks of Eagle Peak was more than I could cope with, so I placed an ice–screw in the glaze covering them and abseiled off, in the process dislodging my sunglasses, which slithered away in the direction of Westland.

Maunga Ma's summit, when I reached it, was enveloped in cloud. It was wide and snowy, making it difficult to see where solid mountain gave way to mist; in all directions there was only whiteness of varying densities. This was a new source of anxiety. The previous day from the glacier below, I had noticed that near the top of my proposed descent route the summit of Maunga Ma was fringed with big snow cornices. Now I could not even tell where the edge of the summit snowfield was, let alone the dividing line between safe ground and treacherous windblown bulges of snow that would collapse as soon as I stood on them. There was not even anything to which I could fasten my rope and pay it out from, in order to crawl towards the edge in the hope of locating the descent route. To look for the way down was too risky.

I dithered around, anxious, uncertain, while the wind began to pick up and cloud kept me blind. Backtracking, I made a couple of half–hearted attempts to find a way down to the east between Maunga Ma and Eagle Peak. But with visibility down to a few metres I did not feel brave; nor was I reassured by the knowledge that for most of the day avalanches had been sweeping the slopes below. So I returned to the summit of Maunga Ma and sat down to consider my situation. It was now six o'clock in the evening: high time to make a decision. Suddenly a hole in the cloud revealed a broad snow slope leading down the western side of the range. It looked straightforward enough; the trouble was I had never heard of anyone climbing Maunga Ma from the west. Yet if I could descend quickly, I might still be able to reach Harpers Rock Bivouac in the Douglas Valley before dark. Up till this point the weather had remained tolerable, but the black clouds driving against the western peaks indicated that a storm could strike at any moment.

The problem was, where to after Harpers Rock? From there out to the West Coast highway would be at least two hard days through some of the roughest terrain in New Zealand. Neither the Douglas Valley nor the Karangarua Valley give easy travelling, especially on an empty stomach, and my meagre food supplies were almost finished. The only other possibility would be to cross into the head of the Landsborough Valley, then travel back to the eastern side of the Divide via the Spence Glacier and Barron Saddle at the head of the Mueller Glacier. There might even be food left in Barron Saddle Hut by climbing parties. This last route, however, would be impossible in bad weather, the others slightly less so.

One problem at a time. The first thing was to get down and find shelter before dark; while hunger remained hypothetical, the danger of being caught up high in a storm was immediate. So I headed west and down, and it turned out to be as easy as it looked. Snow slopes and snow covered rock slabs descended to an easy glacial shelf, which enabled me to traverse left across a basin below Mt Isabel and Awatea Peak. There, with the last vestiges of daylight to help me, I stepped off the final patch of snow, to negotiate a steep–sided ravine by half seeing, half feeling my way along the only ledge across it. On its far side, the feeble rays of a fragment of moon helped me to stumble across a grassy slope, until the west ridge of Mt Thomson across the valley rose and blocked out the light. Now I could see nothing. Below, the slope fell away in blackness, steep and airy. I had the staggers.

It was time to stop. I spread the rope over some rocks and took off my boots, rearranged saturated clothing, then leaned back and began the long wait for dawn. The night turned bitterly cold. Snow flurries blew past me in the darkness. Gradually the clouds disappeared to reveal stars, glittering icily beyond the silhouette of the mountains. I sat facing south, gazing at the Milky Way. When the cold became unbearable I jumped up and down on the spot, flailing my arms until weariness forced me to return to my shivering. Yet at times I did doze, and morning did come, eventually.

At first light I moved off, stiffly, awkwardly, down to the valley floor, buffeted by the wind that blew from the south, strong and icy cold. My feet were extremely sore – boot problems, as usual – so at the corner of the little stony flat leading to Harpers Rock, in the shelter of long silver tussock, I rested, to think over what lay ahead and prepare myself mentally. There I ate a few biscuits, the last food I had. My mind was already made up. Since the weather had cleared, the best option would be to cross Douglas Pass into the Landsborough and make for Barron Saddle Hut. In any event, there would be a comfortable place to sleep, and with a little luck there would also be surplus food left there by other climbers. Then the next day it would be a straightforward walk down the Mueller Glacier to pick up my gear below Eagle Peak.

So I turned left instead of right, climbing steep grass to Douglas Pass and then descending its far side to the moraine hummocks of the McKerrow Glacier. This far I had been before, but when I started down the glacier I was heading into new territory. Around the corner of the valley the glacier gave up its struggle against sun, wind and rain, expiring in a confusion of shattered rock, piles of grey mountain dust ground fine by the ice, and grey pools in which small icebergs rotted. Deep silence gave way to the rush of water, as in one pool the infant Landsborough River emerged from beneath a bank of dirty ice; for a few moments it circled hesitatingly among silt banks and shallows, blinking in sunlight, then got its bearings and started off down the valley in the direction of the Tasman Sea.

On the right, rock walls rose for hundreds of metres, blocking access to the Karangarua Valley; on the left, the disintegrating flank of Mt Burns pressed the young river hard, sliding huge blocks of stone down to the water's edge, where they lay in a dangerous unstable jumble. Not even here, in its infancy, does the Landsborough offer easy passage. Nonetheless, once the river manages to escape Mt Burns' pressure, its valley becomes wider, tussock and scattered scrub appear, and it is possible to walk for brief intervals without watching every step. I found the earth soft and soothing underfoot. It became difficult to resist the temptation to stop and lie down among the sun–warmed silver tussocks, to stretch out and sleep. Yet if I was to get back to the eastern side of the Divide that day, I had to keep on going.

All too soon it was time to leave the river again. I turned left, up Rubicon Torrent, climbing to the Spence Glacier, then up its ice to the smooth rock slabs that rise to the crest of the Main Divide. There was no sign of the slabs at all: everything was the brilliant white of new snow, gleaming flawlessly in the afternoon light. On the steep slope, with unprotected eyes close to the snow, I became worried about snowblindness, so to reduce the glare I wrapped a gauze bandage around my head and over my eyes. Had anyone encountered me they would have had a fright: a lone survivor of some grim mountain tragedy, or an alpine mummy in search of its tomb? Although the new snow was hard on my eyes, it made climbing very easy, providing such a firm cover over the slabs that I could crampon up anywhere.

I reached the crest of the Main Divide, at the gap between Mt Montgomery and Scissors, with daylight to spare, and from there it was only an hour across the head of the Mueller Glacier to Barron Saddle and the hut. There was no one about to frighten with my mummy outfit. The hut was deserted and contained not even a few grains of rice or a crust of bread to take the edge off my hunger. The only fuel for my trip down the glacier the next day was a cup of warm water.

CHAPTER TWO

I'm not a spoil–sport, I would never wish
To interfere with anybody's pleasures;
By all means climb, or hunt, or even fish,
All hearts have ugly little treasures;
But think it time to take repressive measures
When someone says, adopting the 'I know' line,
The Good Life is confined above the snow–line.
  – W. H. Auden, *Letter to Lord Byron*

Was the Eagle Peak excursion successful? Was it an achievement? Perhaps I should cue your response by referring to it as an expedition, for then you could assume that you were meant to respond in terms of triumphing over adversity and hardship, high adventure, adrenalin, mountain conquest, et cetera. Some would say that in the type of activity described the only thing that matters is coming back alive, and if you want a criterion of success, that is it. Now, to be sure, I certainly wouldn't wish to be accused of underestimating the value of staying alive, but the fact is I think we need to set our sights higher.

Suppose we had to give the Eagle Peak expedursion a score. (Climbing has become a competitive sport, done in gymnasiums in front of judges and spectators, and scored, so why not?) Let's give it a minimum score of fifty percent, on the grounds that any mountain journey from which the traveller returns in one piece must be deemed to be at least satisfactory. But how much higher would we be prepared to go?

Should I get more points because it was a first ascent? This would imply that climbing the Mueller Face of Eagle Peak mattered, that in some modest way it represents a new human achievement, a rolling back of the boundaries of the unknown, a triumph of the human spirit. Yet even when qualified as modest, it seems pretentious, not to say absurd, to claim that this mountain journey mattered to anyone but me. Subsequently I mentioned it only to a few friends, and the climb went unrecorded in news bulletins, so even had it mattered in some way, the world at large did not learn of it and continued about its business unaffected by my exploit.

Although Eagle Peak is a nice mountain, its summit is just a bump on the Main Divide, surrounded by higher and more imposing peaks. Unless seen from somewhere to the east, such as the lower Hooker Valley, generally it does not seem significant enough to attract attention. That Eagle Peak arouses interest only on closer acquaintance is clear from its name. After all, there are no eagles in New Zealand, so why Eagle Peak? The answer lies in its appearance. From the nearby southeastern slope of Mt Thomson, at an altitude of a little more than 2000 metres, the summit of the mountain looks like a gigantic eagle gazing along the crest of the Divide, with a folded wing of stone hanging down on each side of the range. It is only from this angle that the eagle is visible, and this is one of the few mountain names in the region that is descriptive, that records an interaction with the landscape rather than an orgy of colonial possession–taking. It appears that the Austrian guide Conrad Kain named Eagle Peak during the first ascent of Mt Thomson in February 1914. It does not surprise me that Kain was impressed enough by the sight of Eagle Peak to return the following year and make an ascent, having done much the same thing myself, only in my case the idea took eleven years to come to fruition.

For me, as for Kain, the wish to climb Eagle Peak was prompted by seeing it at close quarters; and for me, as no doubt for Kain, it also mattered that the route I followed had not been climbed before. The problem was that it mattered too much. I came to the mountain with a plan fixed in my head and persevered against my better judgement; that the conditions were bad made my performance foolish rather than creditable. Sure, I coped with treacherous snow, iced rock and having to traverse unfamiliar and difficult terrain on an empty stomach. The trouble was that the desire to do that first ascent distorted my judgement. I should have been more prudent regarding weather and conditions. I should have thought the situation through, waited for the snow to settle, come back the following week or the following year. Putting myself in a dangerous position and then having to extract myself from it deserves little praise.

Those avalanches really put the wind up me. They stripped me of my self–possession, that sense of control and ease essential for travelling well in the mountains. The fear and tension generated by the avalanches stayed with me, fading perhaps, but later reinforced by the anxieties of having to deal with new territory, stormy weather, hunger and lack of shelter.

What, then, about that comforting presence? Do I deserve extra points for that? Was it a religious experience, a case of intervention by a compassionate deity who, for reasons unknown, thought me worth saving? Certainly it is the only time I have had such an experience, and in this and its clarity it was exceptional. Nonetheless, in mountain travel and exploration such experiences are not uncommon. They are most likely to occur when those involved are in dire straits, alone, suffering from hunger and thirst, and near the limits of endurance. The interpretations, as might be expected, are varied, ranging from religious epiphanies to hallucinations, from psychological projections to the processes of body chemistry. Because it has been a relatively common experience among mountaineers in the high Himalaya, many are inclined to explain the presence as a consequence of hypoxia or oxygen starvation, which seriously impairs perception and thought processes.

In Himalayan accounts, experience of the presence is often placed under the general heading of hallucinations, the distortions of perception and cognition which are the almost routine consequences of the combined effects of hypoxia, dehydration and exhaustion. Yet those who experience the presence tend to regard it as something separate and distinctive, rather than a mental derangement. It is not confusing, misleading or unsettling; on the contrary, it seems right, appropriate and, above all, sane; it helps those who encounter it to get a grip on themselves and the situation, and aids rather than undermines their decision making capacity. It is precisely what is needed in the circumstances.

In 1915 Ernest Shackleton and two companions crossed the mountains of South Georgia, following a desperate journey by open boat from Elephant Island to bring relief to the members of his expedition stranded there. For thirty–six hours, with scant supplies, little rest and Antarctic winter setting in, they traversed completely unfamiliar mountains and glaciers, knowing all too well that that their own lives and those of twenty–five others depended on their ability to reach a whaling station on the northeastern coastline. On this journey Shackleton sensed that he had not two companions, but three; in addition to Frank Worsley and Tom Crean, there was a presence that supported and guided them. After their journey was over, both Worsley and Crean told Shackleton, independently, that they too had sensed an extra member in their party. Shackleton was convinced that theirs was a religious experience, an apprehension of the 'Providence' he was certain had watched over his expedition members throughout their nineteen–month ordeal.

In the case of Shackleton's party, three men had what seems to have been the same experience, though we cannot actually say that they shared a common experience. Does this amount to proof that there was something 'out there' – the Almighty, say, in Edwardian garb: tweed suit, collar and tie, imposing yet modest, not altogether clear in his instructions or what he was about?

In 1953 the Austrian climber Hermann Buhl spent a night out at 8000 metres on Nanga Parbat, the ninth highest mountain in the world, following his solo push to the summit to make the first ascent. When descending the following day, he also had a feeling that he was not alone. He sensed there was someone with him who was looking after him, a sort of invisible climbing partner linked to him by a invisible rope. In his subsequent account of the climb, Buhl treated the experience sceptically: 'I knew it was imagination', he wrote, 'but the feeling persisted.' Although the presence calmed him and made him feel more secure, Buhl claimed to have regarded it as an illusion, one which, should he have given in to it, might have undermined his heedfulness, his sense of sole responsibility for his every move; only by forcing himself to acknowledge the reality of his solitude did he remain watchful and self–reliant enough to get down alive.

Reinhold Messner, the first person to climb all fourteen 8000 metre peaks, had similar experiences on Nanga Parbat. In 1970, with his brother Günter, he reached the summit by the Rupal Face and then descended the largely unknown Diamir Face, without food, water, or equipment, over several days. During the descent, near the end of which Günter was to be engulfed by an avalanche, Reinhold sensed an additional presence, one that he felt was always situated just outside his field of vision. In 1978, when he returned to make the first ascent of the face that had taken his brother's life, Messner again sensed that presence. It guided him on difficult sections of the climb, telling him which way to move in order to avoid obstacles. Near the summit he found himself talking to the presence, which continued to reassure him, and although it remained beyond his field of vision, he had the impression that he was communicating with a girl. In a similar way, high on Mt Everest in 1933, the English climber Frank Smythe found himself offering a piece of mint cake to a presence that had accompanied him all day, yet remained, as always, invisible.

The Australian climber Greg Child, who has written an essay on 'the other presence', describes a terrible descent of Broad Peak in the Karakoram Range, at night, during a storm, with a companion incapacitated by pulmonary oedema. Child sensed at times both that he was outside his own body, observing the events, and that there was someone watching over his shoulder. As conditions continued to deteriorate, he felt that the other presence was guiding their descent, checking every move and every decision until the pair reached their tent at two o'clock in the morning.

There is no self–evident reason for assuming that 'the presence' experienced by myself and others is the same in each case. To assume that would be to presuppose a particular kind of answer to the questions posed by the phenomenon. However, the descriptions given by Messner and Child, for example, fit my own experience quite well. Although I feel no need at all to personify the presence, I too had an awareness of something that could be described as situated just outside my field of vision, behind my shoulder, and that this impression blurred, at least part of the time, with a sense of being somehow located there myself, observing myself and my predicament 'objectively', so to speak. I will go further and say that it was always behind my right shoulder, never my left. Perhaps that is significant, if we are inclined to look for explanations in the reasoning and regulative functions of the left hemisphere of the brain.

Certainly for me the experience of the presence was exceptional. It was unlooked for, unexpected, as if I had crossed a threshold into a strange hall, still and soothing. But no, that is not right; the impact was far more dramatic than that: it was as if a wall had suddenly disappeared and I was suspended in the air outside a tall building, able to see what myself and others were doing inside. Yet if the experience was dramatically novel, it was also somehow familiar; it was not disturbing but reassuring and comforting. There was no bliss or ecstasy, of the sort usually said to be characteristic of mystical experiences, only calmness and clarity, a sense of security and control.

Attempts to explain the experience in terms of hypoxia and brain chemistry are not very convincing. After all, Shackleton and his companions were not far above sea level in South Georgia, while on Eagle Peak I was at a height of less than 2500 metres, and whatever problems I may have encountered, lack of oxygen was not one of them. Perhaps hypoxia does make the experience of a presence more likely than at lower altitudes, as seems to be the case with hallucinations. However, it obviously is not a necessary condition and it cannot be an adequate explanation in itself. And neither can my experience be explained as a consequence of dehydration, hunger or exhaustion. It was at most five or six hours since I had eaten a good meal and I was not particularly tired: my throat was dry, true, after my fright with the avalanches, but I have been much thirstier without having similar experiences.

How about fear then, or awareness of being in extremis? While those avalanches gave me a bad case of the shakes, by the time the presence made itself felt I had reached the upper rocks of the face and knew I was on secure ground; I still felt extremely nervous, to be sure, but I was no longer at desperation point. Death only gave me a bit of a nudge with that sliding snow, it did not stay around to stare me in the face.

Maybe what this all indicates is that I have a lower breaking point than others, am more inclined to freak out, short circuit or scream for help, psychically as well as vocally. However, that has not been my general experience. Not surprisingly, I am attracted to the opposite explanation: perhaps those who experience the presence (especially at low altitudes) have relatively strongly developed 'governors', personal control mechanisms that somehow manage to change into a higher gear in moments of extreme need and take charge. It is as if reason manages to project and objectify itself, telling the emotions that there is no need for all this carry–on, that the thing can be done if only the self will pull itself together. Of course this doesn't answer the question of how our critical faculty knows the way up or down unfamiliar mountains. The answer could be that with a cool head we are much better at picking up clues from our surroundings than we appreciate. Further, there is no reason to assume that the presence really is infallible in its guidance and decision making; maybe it is simply that when it makes a mistake the climber or explorer does not return to tell the story.

Although I am inclined to accept the sort of psychological explanation that some like to express in terms of dissociation of personality, there do not appear to be clear evidential reasons for rejecting other sorts of explanations. It depends to a large extent on one's starting point and the cultural or intellectual assumptions one brings to the experience. Had I a more religious outlook, or had the experience taken place in the context of life in a religious community, no doubt I would have regarded it as a powerful demonstration of God's love and compassion. I might be tempted to draw parallels between the privations experienced in hostile environments and religious traditions of fasting and seclusion in order to draw closer to God.

Some see the presence as the spirits of the dead demonstrating their continuing concern and support for the living. Who knows what the dead can or cannot do, or the sorts of constraints to which they might be subject when intervening in mortal affairs? It has been suggested to me that the presence on Eagle Peak might have been the spirit of my friend Bruce Jenkinson, who was killed nearby in a climbing accident in 1973. I am sure that from the next world Jenk would be as quick to help a friend as he was in this one, for he had a strong sense of responsibility, especially for those with whom he went into the mountains. However, the presence certainly did not identify itself as anyone in particular, and I imagine that had Bruce in fact found it possible to cross over and come to my assistance, he would have stuck around a bit longer and not disappeared without saying hello.

There are other possible explanations outside the dominant intellectual traditions of the West, arising in systems of thought such as Taoism, Hinduism, Buddhism, and various shamanistic traditions. These would involve interpreting the presence as a manifestation of the spiritual power of the particular place itself – the mountain, say, or certain trees in a forest nearby. In these traditions, mountains, or specific locations on them, are regarded as places of spiritual potency whose power may be tapped by those who have prepared correctly. Those unconvinced by the argument that experiences of the presence in the high Himalaya are a result of hypoxia and dehydration, for example, may find this sort of account more acceptable.

The evidence regarding experience of the presence is too limited for us to do much more than choose the sort of explanation that fits best with the assumptions we bring to it. As far as my experience on Eagle Peak was concerned, it did not change my life. Interesting, I said to myself later, then almost forgot about it. Nevertheless, it did leave me with a heightened sense of wonder, a greater appreciation that there are many things in this world we do not understand and that we live in a landscape more fascinating than commonsense would have us believe. What is clear is that, no matter how we may prefer to account for the presence, we can claim little credit for it, and I cannot pretend to the world that my ascent of Eagle Peak was a success because I encountered it.

Then there is the other aspect of the Eagle Peak excursion: the business of going into the mountains alone. Most tend to regard this as reprehensible rather than praiseworthy. It is dangerous, they say, it is difficult to protect yourself and you endanger others when they have to come to rescue you. When you break a leg or fall down a crevasse, who will go for help? Venturing into the mountains without companions is foolhardy and irresponsible, it ignores the most fundamental rules of safety and commonsense. Go out alone and you get what you deserve.

It cannot be denied that there are many dangers in the mountains and that there are situations where skilled and supportive friends would be most welcome. Yet it is a serious error to believe, to want to believe, that all dangers can be overcome with companions. Some kinds of danger are intensified by making mountain travel a social activity, and there are lots of advantages in going alone.

Working as a mountain guide, as I have done from time to time, does not confer much in the way of material benefit. One lesson it drives home forcefully, however, is that there are worse things than being alone in the mountains. Mountain fatalities, you soon become sharply aware, tend to happen to pairs or even larger numbers. Fastened to a rope with people whose skills and judgement are uncertain, you realise that unwavering concentration, eyes in the back of your head and a lot of luck still may not be enough to keep you out of trouble. When guiding you simply cannot afford to make mistakes, so you learn to climb with extreme care and a healthy safety margin. Therefore guiding is good training for solo journeys in the mountains.

Going into the mountains alone gives great flexibility with regard to weather and conditions; you can pick your time and go when circumstances are favourable. This is another reason why my Eagle Peak episode was less than admirable: since I had the flexibility conferred by going alone, I should have shown better judgement and bided my time. What is more, travelling alone in the mountains confers an even greater kind of flexibility: the ability to revise your plans as you go, as well as before setting out. When you are alone, social pressures and expectations fade, even if they do not disappear altogether. What does disappear is the need to convince others that plans should be changed because there may be better options. At least in this sense I was able to re–negotiate my descent from Eagle Peak.

On climbing expeditions, social pressures are often intense, despite the nonconformity affected by climbers. The desire to impress companions and establish a reputation; to hold one's own or at least to save face; to compete and to outdo each other: such motives frequently push mountaineers to attempt what they fear and what they know in their hearts is beyond them. They are pressured into ignoring dangers they would privately acknowledge and persevering even when they know it is foolhardy because nobody wants to be the first to suggest turning back.

The Chinese writer Lu Hsün formulated a phrase that is as pertinent to mountain travel as it is to other potentially dangerous human activities. Reflecting on the execution of the young female revolutionary, Ch'iu Chin, by the Manchu imperial authorities in July 1907, Lu Hsün commented that she had been 'clapped to death'. By that he meant that the applause and encouragement she'd received from an admiring public had led her to become reckless; popular acclaim had undermined her judgement and she threw away her life for nothing. Many a mountaineer has been clapped to death too. This applies to those who feel compelled to perform for their companions no less than those who crave for media attention on their return. If you must have an audience, there is much to be said for leaving it at home.

One of the biggest advantages of being alone in the mountains is that being cautious, or even a coward, becomes an easy and natural thing to do. Since there is no one with you to witness it, cowardice costs you little; you may be a timorous weakling with impunity. Of course there will be no one there to observe and report your heroics either, on those occasions when you do feel confident or compelled to push yourself close to the limit, but you soon realise that this does not make your achievements any less valuable personally. What matters is the knowledge and mastery you gain, the confidence to act on your own decisions without shying away from the possible consequences. If taking responsibility for oneself has any meaning, solo mountaineering is one situation that brings it into sharp focus.

There are many different ways of being in the mountains. Some go to pit themselves against nature or to compete against each other. Others use mountaineering as an excuse for spending time in isolated places, in much the same way that fishermen use fishing as a pretext for doing nothing; they never actually get around to climbing anything, but find great enjoyment in just being there. There are also those interested only in solving 'technical' mountaineering problems, who spend as little time as possible in the mountains, flying in to the foot of a climb and then being whisked out again by air as soon as it is over. What we find depends to a large extent on what we seek.

Of course there are reasons for going into the mountains alone that have nothing to do with calculating risks or strategies for survival. Solitude intensifies experience. It heightens awareness and quickens responsiveness to our surroundings. Being alone also increases the demands the environment makes on us. Those demands are not always or easily met, and if they overwhelm us the dangers become acute. It is the need to meet those demands that is one of the attractions of mountain solitude. The goal is not mindless thrillseeking or a search for ever greater emotional stimuli, but rather training mind and body to achieve greater self–control, and thereby greater freedom.

Being able to move in the mountains deftly, lightly, with a minimum of damage to oneself and to the environment, requires much more than skill at moving over rock and ice; it requires knowledge that can only be acquired gradually by being in the mountain setting and learning to read and respond to its signs. It includes knowledge of the way that mountain ridges shape air currents, and the feel of the air before rain; the impact of global warming on glaciers, and the impact of avalanches on people; how the lie of rock strata and a million years of water flow shape gorges and valley walls, and how an overnight flood can change them dramatically; the effect of wind and winter shadow on forest, and how some types of lichen become slippery when wet; and an understanding of wildlife, or what is left of it. It is knowledge that entails an appreciation of the fact that what occurs below the snowline is just as significant as what occurs beyond it, that each illuminates the other.

The knowledge in question is both physical and intellectual, not always fully conscious or articulated. It is self–knowledge no less than knowledge of the mountain environment. The two come together in a sense of belonging, of feeling at home, of being subject to the same processes of weathering as rocks, trees, moss, and changing along with them. While the acquisition of such knowledge involves the extension of personal mastery and familiarity with new territory, it also entails developing a growing harmony with the environment, even in the most trying circumstances.

What follows are evocations and reflections prompted by a series of journeys undertaken in the mountains of South Westland over a period of some sixteen years, taking the Eagle Peak adventure as my starting point. The journeys themselves were *not* shared; they involved solitary travel through wild and remote places. Solitude was an essential part of the experience.

Usually, when setting out, I had a particular mountaineering objective in mind, though this tended to be incidental to the journey as a whole, on a par with following a river's course or crossing from one side of a range to another. Sometimes those mountaineering plans came off, sometimes not. There were times when I was happy to scuttle past as quietly as I could, content to get out unnoticed and unmolested. What these journeys entailed, above all, was a growing attunement with the landscape of South Westland, a sense of familiarity and understanding built up over time, incorporating hard–won knowledge, scars, strength, equilibrium, love.

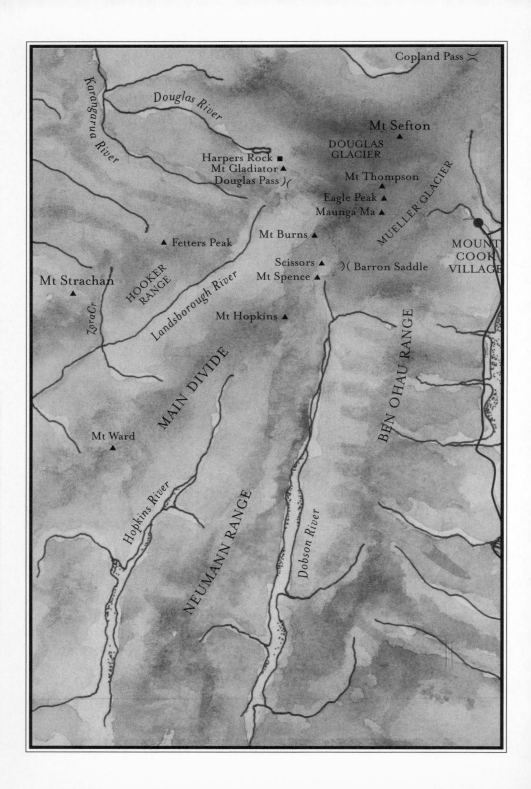

CHAPTER THREE

a boiling, turbulent mountain–torrent.
– Gerhard Mueller
this valley seems to be generally in a state of vapour
– T. N. Brodrick

April 1987. I wanted to go further down the Landsborough River, cross the Solution Range and climb Mt Hooker, then follow the Otoko River down to the West Coast. So there I was, in Barron Saddle Hut again, waiting for the wind to die down, contemplating the pile of food and equipment I would have to carry. After a fierce snowstorm, the surrounding mountains were coated in ice. It looked like the beginning of winter.

Wind has to be taken seriously at Barron Saddle. It lies near the heads of three big valleys – the Mueller and Dobson on the eastern side of the Main Divide, the Landsborough to the west – and the wind blows from all directions, rising suddenly and gusting violently. Among steep rocks and snowdrifts below the saddle, on its Dobson Valley face, lie the remains of the original mountaineering hut here: sheets of corrugated iron, broken timbers, flooring. In February 1977 the entire hut was blown off the saddle with four climbers inside it. On the saddle itself, just back from the edge of the drop, the snapped ends of its anchor cables still nod forlornly on the wind.

There is no easy route into the Landsborough, particularly for those with heavy loads. The route I had followed out of the valley three years earlier, Hardies Gut, presents no problems when there is enough snow to cover its smooth rock slabs, but now those slabs were likely to be coated in ice. Moreover, in the interests of comfort I was wearing soft, bendable hiking boots rather than stiff mountaineering boots, which made the idea of encountering steep ice particularly unpleasant. The original route into the Landsborough from Barron Saddle and the head of the Mueller Glacier was Fyfe Pass, first used by Tom Fyfe and George Graham in 1894. A recent guidebook comments that nowadays this route is rarely used. The descent on the Landsborough side of the pass is down another one of the nasty slabby gullies so common to the area; this one, however, has an additional little surprise in store for those who venture down it. Over the years, the retreat of the ice of the Spence Glacier has exposed overhanging rock where once the gully led out onto easy snow and ice. The fact that the route is 'no longer so popular' probably has something to do with this. Another guidebook advises that the best way into the Landsborough is probably over the top of Mt Spence. Well, Mt Spence is a pleasant climb, but it leads nowhere, and no one in their right mind would consider it as an access route unless a guidebook told them so.

I had been shown the best route into the Landsborough by a big bull thar in February 1964, although I did not understand it at the time. With a companion I was traversing the snow slopes below Scissors, making for the lowpoint on the Main Divide on the way out to Mt Spence. There we saw him. He was peering down from the ridge, with the early morning sun lighting up the blond ruff that framed his dark face, his horns as sharp as the rocks around him, and his long hair quivering on the cold wind that blew out of the shadows of Westland. He stood motionless, broad and muscular against the sky, with a vaguely contemptuous expression on his face as he watched our progress: Amateurs! Then he turned, flashed his rump, and vanished on the Landsborough side of the ridge. When we reached the ridge a few minutes later, we found we could proceed in the direction the thar had taken only by hooking our fingers over the actual crest of the Divide and scuttling along crabwise. It really was most humbling. If ever the expression 'running rings around someone' meant anything, that was the occasion.

Thar are more reliable than guidebooks. They have only lived in the central New Zealand Alps for one hundred years, but they have studied the landscape well. I have learned not to question their judgement. They do not take unnecessary risks, and while sometimes their objectives differ from those of humans, much of the time they are the same. Their skill at route–finding is such that when my decisions coincide with thar mountain sense I feel proud and pleased with myself. Once I was caught by a snowstorm on the valley wall above the head of the Karangarua River. Being unsure of the way down, I decided that caution was the best policy and retreated the way I had come, over Mt Gladiator. With remnants of the storm blowing around me and night closing in, traversing the exposed ridge was nerve-wracking until I noticed thar tracks leading from one rock outcrop to another. All I had to do was follow them. Through whiteout and encroaching night they led down unerringly, taking me along the safest and easiest route all the way to Douglas Pass.

Between Scissors and Mt Spence, where I was given my lesson in mountain movement by that bull thar, there are frequently thar tracks too, climbing straight out of the Dobson Valley to the lowpoint on the ridge. There is no doubt that this is one of their routes across the Main Divide to the Landsborough. So I had a good idea of where to go, at least to that point on the ridge. However, standing on Barron Saddle at midday, bracing myself against buffeting winds, getting there did not look easy. The peaks were plastered with ice and fresh powder snow swirled over the rocks; and with a heavy pack on my back and lightweight boots on my feet the snow slope leading towards the low point looked uncomfortably steep. To avoid it, I climbed directly up the ridge in the direction of Scissors, seeking shelter from the wind on its Mueller side, until wide snowy ledges led left to where the thar cross the range. Then below me lay the Landsborough Valley.

Getting down to the Spence Glacier was surprisingly unstressful, even with my crampons strapped to absurdly bendable boots. Not far down the western side of the Divide a series of snow–covered ledges sloped down to the right, leading to the top of a shattered buttress of rock that in turn gave easy access to the glacier. Away from the top of the range there was no wind and the afternoon sun was warm.

The Spence Glacier has shrunk almost to non–existence; a miserable moraine–covered remnant, it huddles below the wall of Mt Burns and Watch Tower, avoiding the sunlight and trying desperately to stop itself from sliding into its terminal lake. Its final slope was littered with fool's gold, seams of which riddle the rocks that fall from the shoulder of Mt Burns. The 'nuggets' had also been there when I ascended the glacier a few years earlier. I am reasonably confident it was fool's gold: in any event, I didn't pick any of it up, so either way it *was* fool's gold. In 1894 Tom Fyfe and George Graham found it too. George got very excited for a while, thinking their fortunes were made, but no such luck.

From the lake at the end of the glacier I veered left, away from the moraine banks of Rubicon Torrent, looking for softer ground on which to descend, for my feet were getting sore, and so came into what for me was new territory, and the Landsborough Valley proper. Grassy slopes dotted with gentians led down beside a stream to a swampy terrace just above the river. Here, sprawled on the grass beside shallow pools, gazing idly at the mountains, I had my first real rest since leaving Barron Saddle. On the far side of the river, the rocky summits of Mt Townsend and Whitcombe Peak lined the valley, and just downstream rose the barrier of Fettes Peak, its glaciers spilling almost to the valley floor. On my side of the river, to the right, Mt Burns blocked out much of the sky, while to the left the northern wall of Mt McKerrow loomed large and close. In the valley nothing stirred, the autumn sun was warm and the air still except for a faint breeze that now and again carried with it the river's voice.

Crossing the Landsborough proved straightforward, confirming the traditional Westland wisdom of venturing into the mountains when the summer snow melt is over and the glaciers are bare and bony. The water was only thigh–deep and its force withstandable. Nonetheless, my hopes of finding easy walking along a terrace on the true right bank were disappointed, for the valley side was steep and its tussocks slippery. With dusk coming on, I climbed up and down as I went, looking for a dry rock under which to camp, until I eventually stopped for the night under one good for little more than keeping off the dew.

The morning broke with an ominous light: there was a big storm brewing. Mt Burns and the head of the valley had disappeared under cloud that swept in from the northwest; there was no sight of Fettes Peak, which the previous evening had appeared to fill the whole of the valley downstream, and across the river Mt McKerrow had vanished as well. I packed up quickly and continued downstream, keeping close to the river. As I reached the treeline beyond the Fettes Glacier the rain began. It is here, too, that the upper Landsborough gorge begins. The river bed falls away as if weighed down by the massive boulders that choke it; the valley sides grow steeper and closer, hemming the river in with bluffs that force the traveller now to wade in its rushing water, now to sidle high in search of a way through. The rain fell relentlessly, incessantly. Side streams swelled and thundered down to the river, waterfalls spilled over every bluff; the whole valley was awash. The day ceased to have form or shape; it was reduced to a blur of water, slippery rock, wet forest, moss, mist and the roar of the river, through which I had to find my way one step at a time, with infinite care and patience. One moment of distraction due to tiredness or discomfort, one unheedful step, could have grim consequences.

By the time I reached Zora Creek, at the end of the gorge, five or six hours later, I was weary, footsore and anxious. Rain still fell from a windless, featureless sky, looking as if it would continue forever. Evening was coming on, I was wet, had no tent, and the nearest shelter marked on my map was a hut at Kea Flat, still some eight kilometres downstream on the other side of the Landsborough. If I failed to reach that hut it would be a long and miserable night.

Zora Creek was running high and discoloured. Three times, in three different places, I tried to ford it, and three times beat a hasty, waterlogged retreat. Many a party has found itself in trouble here. The list starts with Gerhard Mueller, Charlie Douglas and their survey party, who in 1887 mapped the entire Landsborough basin. They were fortunate enough to find a large boulder in the middle of the Zora, which enabled them to construct a two span bridge across it. Lack of time and the lack of a boulder meant that for me a bridge was not an option. At the same time I remembered Charlie Douglas' shrewd comment that being unable to swim had saved his life many a time, and the sensible teaching that the best way to deal with flooded rivers is to wait for them to go down. Yet I had to cross. Just upstream from where the Zora's waters foamed into the Landsborough, the stream narrowed to five or six meters and its current swerved from my bank to the opposite side. There was no time to lose. I launched myself, pack still on my back, into the deep–running water, and after a few desperate strokes managed to reach the far shore, where I clambered up the bank and set off on trembling legs for Kea Flat.

Now the wind swung to the south and the rain blew in my face. It became colder. Tired, wet and still anxious, I was shivering uncontrollably. But at least now the going was easy and I could step it out; the grass of Hinds Flat was gentle underfoot. Evening fell early under the thick cloud driving up the valley, and the temperature fell still further. Eventually, however, the rain stopped, and by keeping up a good pace I could more or less maintain my body temperature. River flats continued all the way to Dechen Creek, where with the last glimmers of light I was able to cross to the true left bank of the Landsborough, half feeling my way through water already dark with night. The ford was wide and the river flowed quietly here, despite the day's rain.

But it was still a long way to Kea Flat. By torchlight I carried on, stumbling from weariness. Fresh bootmarks in a silt bank lifted my spirits: there must be hunters staying at the hut, so there would be a fire and a hot drink to be had; and not before time, either, for I was running out of steam. At about ten o'clock, feeling that I must have come far enough, with a final surge I hauled myself up a steep bank into some beech forest. By torchlight the trees seemed tall and even darker than the night, but a few steps later I was out in a clearing: I had been right, it was Kea Flat. Tottering with tiredness now, I shambled slowly along the edge of the clearing, looking for the hut. It was not there. I went in the opposite direction. Still nothing. I called loudly as I staggered along, in the hope that the party in the hut would answer and guide me to them. But no reply. Nothing.

I had to stop. I had to eat and sleep. Through the darkness I could see that while the southerly wind was still blowing cloud up the valley, the cloud base had lifted and a patch of luminous grey above the river hinted that the moon was shining above. Beneath a large beech tree was some long grass and leaf litter, surprisingly dry. I unpacked, tipped some white spirits from my fuel bottle onto a heap of twigs and threw down a match. It erupted in a glorious ball of flame that singed my hair. Then I stripped off, crawled into my sleeping bag and began my first serious feed since breakfast. Although sleep came quickly, the night seemed short.

Dawn was clear. Light valley cloud hung over the river and the air was still; it was going to be a fine day. Having reassured myself of that, I rolled over and slept for another hour. To get underway again called for will power that took some mustering. I limped stiffly down the edge of the clearing, shoulders, legs and ankles complaining bitterly after the previous day's exertions. Worst of all, I had a bad case of nappy rash, for my thighs had been rubbed raw by wet shorts. So I hobbled along in my underpants, shivering in the morning cold.

A few hundred metres from where I had camped I found the explanation for the previous night's footprints. At the lower end of the flat, among the trees, was a fly camp occupied by four hunters. They were surprised to see me. On hearing that I had come down the valley and had called out last night on reaching the flat, one replied, 'Oh, it was you. Thought I heard something, but it was our last night here and we were polishing off the grog. Decided it was just the noise of the river.' And as to the missing hut: 'No, there never was a hut here. Cartographical error. You need to get yourself a new map. It was fixed up on the second edition. Like some breakfast? Got to eat everything anyway. The chopper is picking us up at eleven.'

It turned out to be an extended meal. After the previous day's anxieties, the conversation and the eating soothed my nerves. The hunters had come in by helicopter from Glentanner on the Mt Cook road, with supplies for a week. They had all the comforts of home: big tents, stove, generator, lights, lots of food and (until the night before) plenty of beer to wash it down. The middle reaches of the Landsborough are mighty pleasant country, provided you can arrange an easy entry and exit.

I tend to get nervous wandering around in the bush in early autumn, the time of the roar, when deer hunters are particularly likely to be in out of the way places. As a rule, death by drowning or falling seem to be acceptable risks, since with care and skill they can be minimised; being shot because you've been mistaken for a deer, on the other hand, never seems anything less than stupid. On this occasion, however, the only danger I was in at the hands of my hunter friends was death from overeating, for they were liberal with their hospitality. It was not until eleven o'clock that I set off again, as the hunters scurried about doing the last of their packing, one ear cocked for the helicopter.

Once again it was difficult to muster energy or enthusiasm for the journey, only now I had the extra excuse of a bellyfull of canned sausages and baked beans, not normally a major part of my diet. And besides, the sun was warm; the river caught its light and washed it down the rapids, dashing it against stones in the shallows and leaving it to eddy, scintillating, at the water's edge. How different this from the previous day's travelling. A yearning welled in me to sit quietly in a sheltered corner and soak up that solar energy, but I could neither stop nor relax: yesterday's big wet and that non-existent hut had rattled me; I still felt unsure of what lay ahead and not entirely in control. Worse still, my right ankle was sore. Ten years earlier I had broken it while rock-climbing and it had never been quite the same since; if made to work too hard, particularly supporting a heavy load, it was quick to communicate its displeasure. Although the new lightweight boots I was wearing certainly were more comfortable than climbing boots in the bush and the river, I could not ignore the fact that my ankle would have liked more support. What was more, the load I was carrying was causing me to shift a disproportionate share of the weight to my left leg, and that knee was starting feel the strain. It did not bode well.

Still, there was no need to cross the river for a while, so I could shuffle along the true left bank in the sunshine, without having to think about where I was going. Shingle banks alternated with grassy flats, then a track led confidently downstream through the forest. I merely had to follow it, all the way to Toetoe Flat. There, at the edge of the clearing, the sun's bidding became irresistible. I stretched out in the warm grass, resting my feet, smelling autumn in the air and in the earth, grateful for the respite from nappy rash.

Not far upstream, Mt Dechen rose more than 2000 metres above the river, immense, a skimpy shift of valley cloud clinging to its ample buttocks. Across the river were the slopes of the Solution Range, covered in the uniform dark green of beech forest, the treeless crest of the range showing yellow in the sun. Around me the air was still, and the forest too: utterly still, silent, empty. How different it must have been in the days when Maori parties passed this way. Otoatahi, they called the Landsborough, or Pugnacious Weka, alluding perhaps to the character of the river as well as the richness of its birdlife. The Ngai Tahu sometimes used Brodrick Pass, just downstream, when travelling between their settlements in South Westland and the Waitaki Valley on the eastern side of the ranges. If early pakeha accounts are anything to go by, the number and variety of birds in the Landsborough–Haast Valley and its tributaries would have made for luxurious living.

Early explorers of the lower Landsborough, such as Julius von Haast's party in 1863, and William Docherty and George Hassing in 1865, found it easy to live off the land. Docherty and Hassing dined on an extravagance of kakapo, weka, kiwi and kaka, caught with enthusiasm and minimal effort by their dog Spriggins. After crossing the Haast Pass from the Otago diggings, the trio made their way down the Haast river almost to the coastal plain, prospecting as they went. Then they crossed to the true right bank and turned upstream again, past the Haast–Landsborough junction, apparently continuing all the way up the Clarke tributary of the Landsborough, to Marks Flat, and on to what is now called Lower Otoko Pass. Where they went from there is unclear. Some argue that they descended to the Landsborough River, reaching it not that far from where I lay in the sun procrastinating, and then followed the Landsborough back down to the Haast River, to return over Haast Pass the way they had come. It was a journey of three months, yet they never went hungry.

Thirty–one years later, when A. P. Harper and Ruera Te Naihi (alias Bill the Maori) came all the way down the Landsborough from the Karangarua Saddle, they had a hungry time of it. Feral cats and weasels had largely destroyed the birdlife. All they found in abundance, on the flats near the Clarke confluence, were rabbits, another pakeha gift to the environment. By the 1920s, deer from the herds liberated in Otago had crossed the Divide and were well established in the valley. In the following decades, in order to protect the forest, efforts were made to eradicate the deer, with animals being killed by the thousands. It was not until the 1960s, however, and the advent of export–oriented venison hunting using helicopters and light aeroplanes, that the deer population dwindled. At the end of the twentieth century, the only animal present in large numbers was the Australian brushtail possum. As a record of environmental interaction this may appear extreme and not a little insane, yet the evidence from elsewhere suggests that it is merely an average performance. Nonetheless, it would take real imagination to suggest which creatures could be introduced, in the next decade or two, to give the possums a spell and bring about the final destruction of the forest.

However, lying by the Landsborough, I could not let myself get too worked up about the future, could I, when my main objective was to delay crossing the river as long as possible, and avoid climbing over the Solution Range to Marks Flat. My right ankle was still hurting, and while it was no more than 1000 metres to the top of the Solution Range, that heavy pack was going to make it even more painful and stiff. To delay a little longer, I decided to have something to eat, thereby building up my energy and lightening my load at the same time; and while I savoured a few extra minutes of sunshine I thought about the history of my feet and the boots in which they had suffered.

CHAPTER FOUR

He explained to me that to be without shoes is a very serious fault. When war is raging, one had to think of two things before all others: in the first place of one's shoes, in the second place of food to eat; and not vice versa, as the common herd believes, because he who has shoes can search for food, but the inverse is not true. "But the war is over", I objected.... "There is always war", replied Mordo Nahum memorably.
    – Primo Levi, *The Truce*

We sometimes encounter people who can recount their life history in terms of significant historical events; not necessarily their part in those events, but rather in terms of where they were and what they were doing when the events occurred. I cannot do that; what I can do is tell you my life story in terms of the boots I was wearing while history happened around me. In the mountains as in war, boots matter, and I seem to have spent much of my time searching for boots that are comfortable as well technically adequate, that is, able to get me where I want to go and back again without undue suffering. Despite the fact that having broad feet has made this matter more difficult for me than many others, I refuse to pin all the blame on my feet; boot manufacturers have a case to answer too.

Should this discourse on feet and footwear appear excessive, remember that feet are the most basic reality, the true foundation of things. Besides, you will not want me to continue intruding at decisive moments in the narrative with details of what I have got on my feet or how they are feeling. So it will be best to treat this issue up front.

It was in June 1963, in Sydney, that I bought my first pair of mountaineering boots. What brand they were I cannot remember; anyway, I knew nothing about boots or brands then. It was the smart bits of shiny red leather stitched onto the heels that convinced me to buy them. I had planned to go to Tasmania, but my friend Ted Hartley, who was older and understood me better than I understood myself, suggested I go to New Zealand instead; he even gave me the money to buy a boat ticket across the Tasman Sea. (Before I left he also lent me a book – it puzzled me at the time – with a title along the lines of *Classic Mountaineering Accidents in the Alps*. He was a wise head, old Ted, who had done a lot of thinking over the years, including those of the Second World War, which he spent in jail as a conscientious objector.) All I knew was that the mountains in New Zealand were big and snowy, and that I would be there a week later, so I had to get some footwear in a hurry.

Maybe the red heel patches were some sort of code for blisters; certainly those boots generated many, thereby establishing the pattern for the footwear that was to follow. I was wearing them on the spring evening when Derek and I returned to work at Hanmer Forest Camp after a couple of days in the Spenser Mountains. Hoanni yelled from his hut: 'Hey you jokers, guess what. Kennedy's been shot.'

'Go on', replied Derek. 'You're kidding.'

'It's true, I tell you.'

'Bullshit. I'll bet you five quid.'

Hoanni's face flashed a big grin in the lamplight. 'OK', he said, holding out his hand. 'Five quid, you're on.'

Although the shine had long since disappeared from the red patches, the boots themselves lasted about four months after that. They fell to bits towards the end of my first season in the Mt Cook area, in fact, just before I arranged to climb Mt Spence with a student who had been working over the summer as a glacier guide for the Hermitage Hotel. One of his tasks was to fit hotel guests with boots before they ventured out onto the ice, so it was no problem to fit me with a pair as well. They were standard kiwi farm boots: big, clumsy, stiff and unyielding in all the wrong places, rather like rubber-soled concrete blocks. Still, they were free and in one piece, and remained that way until I left them behind in the toolshed of a derelict gold mine in the Northern Territory. The last time I saw them a lizard had already moved into the right boot and was gazing out of it possessively.

According to Nietzsche the only things that stick in the memory are those branded there by pain. He must be wrong, though, for I remember clearly the Dolomite boots I bought in 1964, and I remember them with affection. They gave me many months of comfortable travelling; in fact, they were the only mountaineering boots I ever had re–soled, and when they and I went our separate ways, literally, about three years later, it was to be a long time before my feet were happy again. Actually they were ski mountaineering boots, with lugs at the front of the soles to fit ski bindings, so to make them suitable for serious climbing I had to round the lugs off with a file. But then they were perfect. Part of the secret was a generous number of leather layers between my feet and the rubber soles, which kept them reasonably stiff while at the same time providing extra cushioning.

I had the Dolomites on my feet the first time I ever visited South Westland. It was December 1964, when with Nigel (alias Bruce) Harrison and Nick von Tunzelmann I crossed Baker Saddle from the Hooker Glacier into the Strauchon Valley. In heavy rain we negotiated the thick scrub and enormous boulders of the Strauchon Gorge. I did not have a clue where we were going; until Nigel and Nick asked me to come with them, back at Mt Cook Village, I had never given much thought to what lay on the western side of the Divide.

We managed to cross the Copland River just upstream of its junction with the Strauchon River by abseiling down the face of a boulder that lay right across it, then scrambled up a small scree slope to the edge of the terrace overlooking the river. Here Nigel and Nick began to get agitated. We looked for the Copland Valley track but could not find it. They had been down the track before and knew it was there somewhere between the edge of the terrace and the cliffs of the valley wall, yet there we were, thrashing about in wet bush to no avail, with daylight running out. We sat down to compose ourselves and puzzle things out. When I mentioned that I had seen a small cairn halfway up the scree slope from the river, Nigel and Nick both turned on me: 'For God's sake, why didn't you say so earlier?' Rather hurt, I muttered to myself, 'You're the ones who are supposed to know where we are going. I figured you must have seen the cairn too.'

The track was there. Within a couple of minutes we reached Tekano Stream, and just on the other side was Douglas Rock Hut. As evening fell, the weather cleared and the cloud lifted to reveal the north ridge of Mt Sefton, which we had come to climb. It looked scary to me: vertical rock that seemed to go on forever, capped somewhere near the skyline by an ice cliff. My companions reassured me that it did not go on forever, that it was only 2000 metres, but I knew enough to realise that 2000 vertical metres is a long way. Nor did the knowledge that nobody had been up there before make me feel better: I could *see* why not.

When we set off before dawn the next day I was not feeling brave, and so was rather relieved when we lost the track on the way to our starting point. It disappeared near Flashing Stream, inflicting on us in the dark a wrestling match with wet scrub. Unfortunately my relief was not to last long after our premature return to the hut an hour later. 'We'll try again at first light', said Nigel.

At six o'clock, when we set off again, I was feeling a little better; daylight makes a difference to the pusillanimous. Now, at least, we could see where we were going, and, as so often happens, the terrain turned out to be much less steep and much easier than it had looked from below. Even without a rope, it was carefree climbing. Below, on our left, a large herd of thar romped on the Fiddian Glacier, apparently enjoying themselves as much as we were. By the time we had reached the ice–cap, however, the weather was closing in again as cloud rolled in from the sea. When we reached the summit, at three o'clock in the afternoon, there was just time for a glimpse down the East Face in the direction of the Mueller Glacier and Mt Cook Village before our surroundings disappeared in the cloud blown at us by the rising northwest wind.

Now we had to find our way down again, something that in bad weather has troubled many a climbing party on the western slopes of Mt Sefton. A mistake in navigation here, with the Copland Valley far below on the right and the precipitous Douglas Neve on the left, costs dearly. But it all went well; descending the snowy west ridge in a whiteout, we came to a gap we guessed to be the key to the way down: Welcome Pass. No sooner had we begun to head down the slope on the Copland side of the range than we emerged from the bottom of the cloud ... to discover that we were indeed at the top of the Tekano Glacier, as we had hoped. Now the rain started again. Our tracks triggered off wet snow avalanches all the way across the head of the glacier, until finally we came to the head of Scotts Creek and could run down grass, rocks, and streams, with the rain pouring down, to beat night to the valley floor. Darkness overtook us as we stumbled wearily up the track back to Douglas Rock. Towards morning, lying semi–conscious in our bunks, we could still think coherently enough to understand that the drumming on the roof was heavy nor'west rain, which meant that it would be impossible to move on the next day, and so surrendered thankfully to sleep again.

In retrospect, what strikes me most is not the magnificence of the deed, of which I found it easy to convince myself at the time, but rather the fact I did not have sore feet at the end of it. After more than 2000 metres up and down over rock, ice, grass and scrub, and wet most of the time, I could still stand more or less unaided. Unfortunately, somewhere towards the end of the 1960s the idea of comfortable all–round mountaineering boots disappeared from view: the age of technological specialisation hit with a vengeance.

But I still have to report what happened to my faithful Dolomites. In August 1967 a windslab avalanche took me over a bluff in the upper Haast Glacier. When I regained consciousness, lying in the snow below it, there was no sight of my pack, in which were the Dolomites and my copy of *Ulysses*. So the boots are still moving around in the mountains. According to my calculations, although they probably reached the Tasman Glacier some years ago, it will still be many more before they reach its terminal face and begin the long voyage down the Tasman River to Lake Pukaki.

It was in 1972, in London, that I acquired a pair of Super RDs, with which the expression 'hard wearing' took on new meaning. Henceforth it would be a matter of breaking in feet to fit boots rather than the other way around. In a way they were emblematic of the spirit of the time: the parting of the ways between the mainstream and the counter–culture; technological mastery had become detached from ordinary sensibility, power from flower. Anyhow, that was how it seemed at the time, and it was certainly how my feet experienced it. My heels left a trail of blood over the Alps that the locals will still be trying to scrub away. Super RDs were good for technical climbing – neat fit, precise, rigid – they were just impossible to walk in. Even when they no longer gave me blisters, on every trek out of the hills my feet would ache and cry out for mercy.

When after much suffering I had finally reached some sort of compromise with them, the heels of the boots started to fall to bits and had to be re–stitched. This was at the end of 1974, just before the last mountaineering course I instructed on at Mt Cook. The new stitching changed the configuration of the heels, and consequently my heels had to be reconfigured too; they ended up with blood poisoning and I was little use as instructor. Eighteen months later, in Tasmania, I finally lost patience with those RDs, swore at René Desmaison for one last time, and left them on the Pine Valley track, completing the rest of the journey over Mt Geryon and home again in rock climbing shoes and bare feet.

But worse was to come. If Monsieur RD had been cursed periodically, the famous French climber whose name was inscribed on the double boots I made the mistake of buying in 1982 was cursed perennially – up hill and down dale. Although I have managed to obliterate from memory the name of both the manufacturer and the endorser, the recollection of a journey through the upper reaches of the Arawata and Joe Rivers remains indelible. Plans of traversing the Olivine Ice Plateau had to be scrapped because I was anxious lest my feet become infected and bad weather trap me west of the Main Divide. It was just as well that O'Leary Pass could serve as an escape route into the Dart Valley. When eventually I staggered out to the road–end in the Matukituki Valley, Janette claimed she could see daylight through my heels. Or was it only bone? It could have been either, the way I was feeling. A couple of years later I did my second and final excursion in those boots: the traverse of Eagle Peak. Had I not been so hungry at the time, and so eager to get home, I am sure I would have paid more attention to the discomfort in locomotion they inflicted.

It was in reaction to those double boots that I had turned to the items on my feet as I lounged in the autumn sun in the Landsborough Valley. They were the opposite end of the spectrum: a pair of lightweight, flexible, cheap, anonymous Italian boots. They were good for walking and splashing through rivers, less good for rock–climbing, and less good still for ice climbing. Comfortable? Yes, but they did not provide much support for my troublesome right ankle, so that towards afternoon I would tend to develop a limp, and on stopping for the evening the ankle would seize up altogether. Still, the boots did more than I could reasonably ask of them, standing up to two hard journeys through the Landsborough. They aged before their time, reduced by constant wet, abrasion and heavy loads to sad misshapen lumps of leather.

It will be no surprise that when my low–tech footwear had to be retired the pendulum swung in the opposite direction again. Although the age of plastic mountaineering boots had dawned long since, thus far I had

41

resisted the trend. It was in autumn 1991 that I finally took the plunge. Wearing purple plastic Koflach boots with green laces, I set off from Mt Cook Village for the Douglas Valley: up the Mueller Glacier, past my bivouac ledge below Eagle Peak, then up the length of the Ngakanoi Glacier and the steep ridge to the summit of Maunga Ma. The ice of the final slope was so hard that I could climb only on the front points of my crampons and was very glad of my stiff plastic boots. On the summit it was hard to believe that this was the same mountain I had been on seven years previously; then it had been a mist–shrouded plateau of snow, now it was a bare ridge of broken rock, warm in the midday sun.

Even with a big load the descent on the western side was as straightforward as I remembered it. The sweat was dripping off me when in mid afternoon I passed the place of my frigid night out, to plod at a leisurely pace down to Harpers Rock Bivouac. Was I pleased with those boots! For the first time in years I wasn't limping at the end of the day. I took the boots off in the shelter and went on bare feet down to the stream to get some water. On the way back, just near the entry to the bivouac, I trod on a sharp stone, tearing the skin off the outside of my little toe. The toe swelled, the plastic boot no longer fitted properly, and when a snowstorm prevented me from crossing into the Karangarua Valley, the best remaining option for getting home was the route I had taken before: across Douglas Pass to the upper Landsborough, then over the range to Barron Saddle. The lower slope of the Spence Glacier was still littered with fool's gold.

This incident rather dented my confidence in the plastic boots. I could not blame them for the injured toe, naturally, but in the end they were still hard, unforgiving pieces of plastic that refused to mould themselves to the shape of my feet. Despite being quite good for steep climbing, they were big and unwieldy. Because of my broad feet, to get them to fit width–wise I had to get them a size too big length–wise; the result was that they made me feel clumsy on broken ground. While my brain would register the fact that my foot had to change direction as it descended, the weight and bulk of the boot would prevent the foot from responding in time, the boot edge would catch on the rock or tree root, and over I would go again.

Clearly, for the sort of travelling I was doing in South Westland, I wanted to be able to have my cake and eat it too: footwear that was adequate from a technical mountaineering point of view, yet comfortable enough for slogging through bush and river gorges. One possible solution was to take two pairs. The plastics were going to take a bit of wearing out, so they had to have another outing. This time (December 1994) they were carried up the Mahitahi River, before earning their keep by getting me safely along the crest of the Hooker Range to the head of the Otoko Valley, then hanging idly from my pack again while a pair of glorified sneakers ferried us all back down to the West Coast. For reasons that will be obvious this arrangement was less than perfect. Not only did the plastic boots have to be carried up and down the valleys, but the lightweight valley footwear made a recurrence of the limping problem inevitable.

This interminable trouble with boots has sometimes tempted me to give the whole business away. Boot manufacturers seemed to have lost sight of the idea that even on difficult terrain movement should be comfortable as well as controlled. The idea that this shift was in response to market demand is too dismal to contemplate, so at this point I prefer to turn to conspiracy theory for an explanation. Perhaps boot manufacturers have shares in helicopter and ski–plane operations, and so have a vested interest in causing climbers to dread walking in the hills. It is also possible that, for some, mountain travel has become a masochistic exercise in which hardship is an end in itself, with discomfort and useless suffering regarded as measures of the quality of the experience. I have not yet been able to reconcile myself to that idea.

One of the dangers of ageing is often an irritating and frequently baseless nostalgia for the good old days. Were those Dolomites of thirty–five years ago really that comfortable, or was I just a little less inclined to whinge then, more able to put up with the hard knocks? I am reassured on this point by the fact that this story of boots has turned out to have a happy ending. Towards the end of the millennium (I feel as if I have had sore feet for a thousand years) there seems to have been a renaissance in the art of boot making, a revival of the idea that it should be possible to combine technical adequacy with comfort. Does this mark a turning point in civilisation, a glorious synthesis of intellect and sensibility that will make us whole again? My feet have become whole again, anyway, and I am content with that.

Since I acquired a pair of La Sportiva Nepal Tops in 1998 my feet have rediscovered the joy of movement. Although a little on the heavy side, when used with two pairs of inner soles the boots are as comfortable as old fashioned leather–upholstered armchairs (and nearly as high). For technical rock and ice they are outstanding, yet still make it possible to zip about on moraine or in the bush without feeling that you are lugging about a ball and chain.

In February 1999, when the glaciers were more bare and broken than I have ever seen them, I wore the Nepal Tops up the Hooker Glacier to revisit the Strauchon Valley. When the descent from Baker Saddle brought me close to desperation point, the boots provided some of the confidence I was personally lacking. Crossing Darkwater Saddle and descending the gorge of Ruera River, they again did me proud, and on reaching Welcome Flat Hut I could still stand on my own two feet. It has not always been like that.

Alex Miller reckons that I am the only person he knows who, on cleaning boots out at the end of a trip, has to dispose of blood. Perhaps he exaggerates; in any case, I hope the future will prove less gory.

CHAPTER FIVE

The men and women of the early colonial era who got their names in history books are the men and women who kept journals, prepared reminiscences, wrote letters or had others record their deeds. Who knows but on every occasion when we say, "This is the pass discovered by Julius Haast in 1863", some old–timer is not revolving in his grave! Our mythical old–timer knows darned well that he crossed Haast pass in 1861, reached the coast, spat in the Tasman, boiled the billy and returned to a claim on the Otago diggings: but he couldn't write, and he'd found no gold so he didn't tell anybody; and shortly afterwards he dropped down a shaft and was killed. It is with the written records left behind by the literate few that the historian perforce must deal...
– Philip Ross May, *The West Coast Gold Rushes*

I could procrastinate no longer. The day was getting on and Marks Flat was still a long way off. The Landsborough River was clear and reflected the blue of the sky, yet despite the lateness of the season it was nearly waist deep, and I was pleased to reach the opposite bank without being up-ended. Open beech forest led up onto a ridge that climbed to the Solution Range. At first there was a deer trail, clear and easy to follow. At the top of a small rise, however, the deer dropped off the right side of the ridge down to a creek, apparently to follow the stream for a while before climbing up the ridge beyond. I was not smart enough to follow them. Higher up, the going on my ridge became less pleasant, with thick windfalls and scrub below the bushline, while above it flax grew on steep rocky knolls. Still, there was no problem really, except that time was ticking by, and already it was late afternoon.

Ice lay in hollows and under rocks amongst the tussock; frost in the air chilled my sweat–soaked clothes and pressed against my forehead like

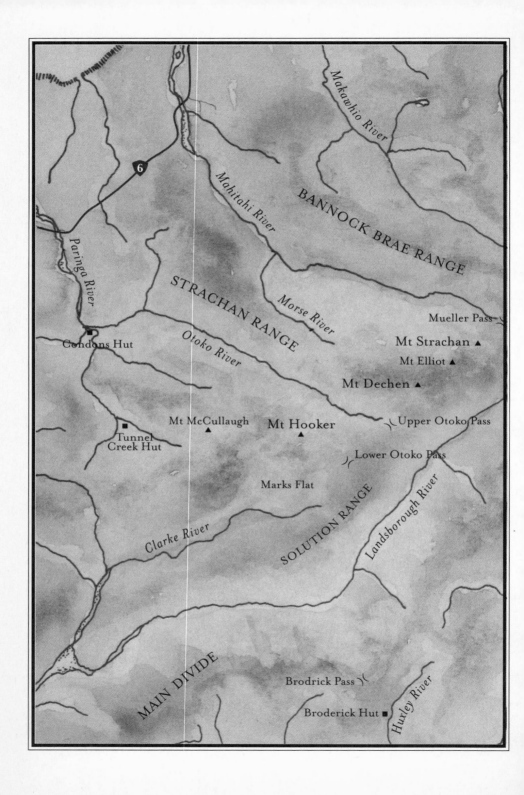

cold metal. Shivering, I looked around uneasily at the shadows deepening around me, regretting now my late departure from Kea Flat. I would be running out of daylight again. Behind me, on the far side of the Landsborough, the setting sun had begun to colour the peaks of the Main Divide.

A little further up the slope a large deer trail crossed my route, climbing at an easy angle from the treeline on my left towards the crest of the Solution Range, where it continued in the direction of Lower Otoko Pass and Westland. It was an old trail, deeply entrenched in places, and though in a state of disrepair it still cut a wide swathe through the tusssock, testimony to the enormous herds that travelled this way before the advent of aerial venison operations in the 1960s.

When I reached the crest the sun was low in the sky. Mt Hooker rose in front of me, high, imposing and sombre in the evening light, its glaciers catching the sun's last rays. At the foot of the mountain Marks Flat lay deep in shadow, already collecting in its basin the cold air washing down from the icefields above. The descent was easy, complicated only by my painful ankle and the slipperiness of tussock blades on the ground. Half limping, half slithering, I headed down the open hillside to the top of a small beech–covered ridge, then groped my way down through forest and deepening darkness to emerge on the flat with the night.

The map showed a bivouac rock at the far end of the flat, two kilometres away, near where the young Clarke River begins the descent through its gorges. Ahead of me in the dark I could see a lowpoint on the horizon that could only be the river's exit from the flat, so steered in that direction as best I could. On my right Mt Hooker walled off the sky, on my left the Kea Cliffs tried hard to equal it. But there was no time to gaze at the stars; in the darkness I was falling over large tussocks and into the mud and water in between. It was icy cold. I felt forlorn and more than a little irritated. Others had always said that Marks Flat was a beautiful place; nothing I'd heard had prepared me for this experience. Veering further towards Mt Hooker, I struck one of the streams that meanders across the flat. Splashing down the stream was easier than tripping over tussocks in the dark, so that was how I continued, tense with cold, whimpering at my sore ankle and nappy rash, overwhelmed by tiredness, my late arrival and my surroundings.

The stream became bigger, its pools deeper, its bed stonier. When I reached the edge of the flat I knew it could not be far to the bivouac, but I had had enough. Already frost lay heavy on the grass and the air itself congealed from the cold. At the first boulder that offered a suggestion of shelter from the frost I stopped and threw down my pack. Once inside my sleeping bag, with water heating on the stove close by, I felt more cheerful, though too tired to prepare a meal. A hot drink and a cold snack would have to do. I just wanted to rest.

Tired though I was, I found it difficult to sleep. My ankle was hurting. I tossed and turned on the frosty ground, dozed, then turned some more. Around midnight I sat up. The moon had risen above the Solution Range and lit up the flat. Ice crystals glittered on the tussock blades. Above the stream a faint mist hovered; there it condensed, descended slowly, then dissolved again on the rippling surface of the stream, also silvered by moonlight. The sound of water eddying about the stones merged with the moonlight and frost, accentuating the heaviness of surrounding mountain shadows, deepening the solitude and the silence.

I thought of William Docherty, George Hassing and Spriggins, camped somewhere near here in the autumn of 1865. It was not hard to imagine them, men and dog, shivering under torn blankets, waiting for morning, their fire of damp twigs long since out and the wind whistling over early snowdrifts between the rocks.

It takes only a little more effort to see a figure sitting opposite me in the moonshadow of a boulder.

'Bill Docherty, is that you?' The figure bows politely and raises its wide–brimmed hat, stepping forward into the moonshine. He is tall, well built, with a full beard and unkempt hair falling down to his shoulders. A tattered oilskin and ragged trousers hang loose about him.

'What are you doing here Bill? You've been dead for ninety years or more.'

He grins. 'I'm not likely to forget that, now, am I? You needed company, so I came. Never mind that it takes some effort. Rather akin to having to go back up a long scree slope after you've come down it.'

'What's it like – being dead, I mean?' (I have not had much experience of this sort of conversation.)

He scratches his beard. 'Well, it sure requires a lot less effort than working for a living. Rather like sitting under a bivvy rock in Westland, really, waiting for the rain to clear, only it never stops. But it certainly makes it easier to stay away from the demon drink.'

'What do you think of the landscape now', I venture, 'after so long an absence?'

'I like it well enough. We always have a soft spot for where we find ourselves, so to speak. The journey with Hassing was my first long prospecting trip hereabouts, and I found I was good at it. Thirty–five I was then, and I kept it up for another thirty years. Towards the end it became harder, but it is no easy thing to change the habits of a lifetime.'

'You didn't find much though, did you?'

'Didn't find much?' He looks hurt. 'If it's gold you are talking about, or just our trip of 1865, you would be close to the mark. But there were things other than gold to find and there were many other journeys. I was a good prospector and knew what I was about, not some fool new chum with pressed shirts and blisters on his hands. I found all I needed to live as I wanted to live. Is that success or not? I found not much gold, true, but there was coal, copper, graphite, lithographic stone, nickel, asbestos. I had money enough, most of the time.'

'Bill, I don't doubt your ability. The truth is, nobody wrote much about you. Of course, that was largely because you were out on your own so much of the time. Finding out what you did is not easy. In fact, even where you are mentioned, it is hard to tell that it is you because the spelling of your name keeps changing. Mostly Docherty, but Haast put you on the map as Doherty, whereas Andreas Reishek, the Austrian bird man you loaned your hut in Dusky Sound, refers to you as "Mr Dougherty, the owner of some west coast coal mines". One historian of New Zealand exploration refers to your 1865 party as "a Danish gold prospector, a companion and dog". Having worked out that the companion in question was you, I always thought you'd been hard done by. Still, at least you were mentioned before the dog.'

He laughs. 'An Irish name married to a Scotch pronunciation, that was the problem. But you mind what you say about that dog. I don't mind him getting more puff than me. Spriggins was a fine animal who kept us stocked with birds. Thanks to him, we ate well. Besides, it was Hassing who wrote up our exploration, so it follows that he got more credit from folks later on. Those who push the pen win out in the end when those who told it differently are pushing up the daisies. Not that George really had that much to say. *The Memory Log of G. M. Hassing*, he called it. Memory block, more like!'

'It was quite some time after your Clarke and Landsborough journey that you went down to Dusky Sound, wasn't it? Then you lived there for many years.'

'True. Some twenty years or so, and most of it on my own, though at first I spent part of the winters in Dunedin. After our journey here, George Hassing and I tried our luck on the beaches around Okarito, when the rush started there. He tired of prospecting and went back to Otago, while I stayed on with Spriggins. It was some ten years after, on my reckoning, that I began prospecting at Dusky. By that time coping with polite society, even West Coast society, had become a chore. In the end I got a bit sandfly happy. The bush is not kind to old stagers. You have to know when to quit.'

'I read somewhere about your final departure from Dusky Sound for Preservation Inlet in an open dinghy tied together with wire and string. It was Richard Henry, wasn't it, who saw you off. He had not long arrived in Dusky, hoping to save ground birds from weasels and stoats by transferring them to Resolution Island. He later complained that when it was time to go you took his whisky bottle with you.'

'Oh, so young Henry did that, did he?' Bill grins at the memory, passing his tongue over his lips. 'You wouldn't happen to have a drop on you now, I suppose, there in that fancy swag of yours? There's none where I am now. Been there ninety years and I still haven't found a way around the rules. Packed with bureaucrats and economists it is, and under new management. Call themselves economic ration–stealers, or something. User pays for everything. The place has gone to the dogs.'

There is no whisky with which to hold his company, so I try to keep the conversation flowing: 'I've heard it said that when you left Dusky you still had hopes of striking it rich at the Cromarty field in Preservation Inlet.'

'No, that was not the way of it at all. I was sixty–four years old and tired. I knew I did not have long to go and wanted company at the end. The Cromarty diggers provided that, and when I died they gave me as fine a send off as a man could want. They buried me on Cemetery Island; a pretty place, where I could listen to the sea, and wood pigeons flying through the forest.'

'When anyone mentions you these days, Bill, it's usually to say you led a lonely life. But you're saying that you stayed in the hills alone because you wanted to, not because you had to?'

'Of course. Naturally. Isn't it the same for you? I learnt early in my prospecting career that it was the looking that gave me pleasure. If the finding mattered, that was more to show others that I was good at what I did. Everyone needs some measure of success. As to exploiting my finds, that mattered much less to me. It was a bloody nuisance. I was not the man for all that overseeing, finance, paperwork. Let others do that. So I made it a habit to sell my finds, pocket the money, and start looking elsewhere. I say there is no life to equal that of travelling in a new country and being free.'

Bill is warming to his topic now and carrying me along with him. I stop trying to put words into his mouth.

'The lithographic stone quarry I started at Abbey Rocks, off the coast near Paringa, brought me three thousand pounds for a half share, which in those days was a tidy sum. For a while in the 1870s the government had hopes that it would be a major vehicle for encouraging settlement in South Westland. My Dusky Sound copper deposit brought me another thousand. Which was a canny deal, as it happened, for although it was high–grade ore, sure enough, in two weeks the whole lode was worked out, and that was the end of it. So I continued my looking, without an urgent need to find.

'In the space of thirty years I travelled a lot of country. First the Gabriels Gully rush in Otago pushed me into the Landsborough and onto the Coast, then in no time the Coast was swamped with diggers and I had the urge to move on again to Dusky. Yet, to tell it straight, for me the problem was not the number of diggers so much as the number of grog shops. I could go without as long as anyone, but once I put my lips to the bottle it required a crowbar to prise them free. Many was the publican between Hokitika and Dunedin that I kept in business. You know how it goes. In a town like Okarito, drinking was the only social activity available; no more hope of your cultural pursuits there than of organising a temperance society. It was a case of drink with others or talk to yourself in a corner, and if you drank you didn't even have to choose.

'Mind, the drink taught me that a man should go where he cannot be tempted. I was neither the first nor the last to stay off the grog by putting a mountain range and a river gorge between myself and the publican's wares. I knew I was a good prospector and bushman, a hopeless townsman and a terrible drunk. If at times I was lonely or the nights were cold and wet, I could always think of a reason for staying where I was.'

'Tell me, Bill. It was at Okarito that you got to know Charlie Douglas, wasn't it?'

'Aye, that's right. Fellow Scot, fellow traveller, fellow drunk. Sometimes Charlie put me in mind of a younger version of myself. We were not always the right influence on each other, me and Charlie. Of course, he was of good stock, as they say, whereas my family was not what would be termed gentlefolk. If it made a difference for Charlie, it was not in the way of making life easier for him. He was of a disposition to see himself as the black sheep of the family. Well, when you are one of a family of black sheep, as I was, you blend in with the crowd and regard yourself as ordinary. The trouble with Charlie was that he was an educated man and inclined to think too much.

'Have you heard about the journey me and Charlie made with Doctor Haast the geologist, in the early Okarito days? You have? Well, you know then that it was when Haast was mapping the coastline, with the three of us in a wee boat no bigger than your hat. A westerly blew up and she just kept blowing. We managed to beach hard by Arnott Point. The problem was, with the way the sea was running, even at ebb tide there was little beach to speak of, never mind when the tide was in. It went on like that for nine days before we could get our little boat out through the breakers and return to Bruce Bay. There were times when I thought Charlie might commit a homicide upon the Doctor, except he was a peaceable chappie.

'Haast believed he was a man of standing, and so he was. Provincial geologist and pillar of the Christchurch community. He liked to have social distinctions observed. A generous man, certainly, but one who wanted to be seen as generous, and used his generosity as a lever for getting others to help him. Well, I was used to dealing with folks like that. I could tug my forelock as required, or flatter them, especially when they might prove helpful later on. But Charlie could not bear being talked down to by anyone, the more so for thinking he had as much book learning as the doctor anyway. So he would get his own back by hurling quotations at Haast from Lord knows what Greek or Roman long–deceased. And when the Doctor asked to be carried across a creek, Charlie dropped him right in the middle.

'I kept in touch with Haast for some time. After all, a provincial geologist is a right handy figure for a prospector to know. He was useful in other ways too. Over the next few years he kept me in rations by paying for bird skins, eggs and the like, and always treated me square. When he opened the provincial museum I sent him a nice slab of lithographic stone from Abbey Rocks to exhibit.

'Naturally, he was interested in where Hassing and I had got to back in '65, here in the Clarke and the Landsborough. When not bailing out the boat, I gave him the full story, and on his map of the province the following year he drew in the details like I'd told him. Even put in Docherty Pass, right next to Mt Hooker here.'

'Yes', I interject. 'But he got it wrong, didn't he? He recorded "A pass next to Mt Hooker leading into the Mahitahi", unaware that Mt Dechen and Mt Strachan are in between. No wonder those who came later rubbed out your name and called it Lower Otoko Pass.'

'Now don't you be too hard on the poor fellow. Study his map and you'll see that he drew the pass correctly, leading from the head of the Clarke into the Otoko branch of the Paringa River. In any case, he was going by what I'd told him. In those days nobody had very clear notions as to which way the rivers ran, or if they did they weren't saying. And my mate Hassing's record of our journey wasn't much use, was it? A typical digger's yarn, that one. "Where have you been?" "Oh, out and about." "Find anything?" "Not really..." Get more information out of his dog. Nothing like a prospector's directions to get you lost, particularly when he is writing more than fifty years after the event. For all that Haast's map looks odd now, he put together all we knew at the time pretty well. He was good at that – making use of what others told him. He remembered what I said, including the fact that my pass was only about 500 feet high. And really, how many passes are there around here that match that description?'

'It certainly fits Lower Otoko Pass better than anything else within a kea's flight of here.'

'Naturally, because that's the pass I told him about, same as I told Charlie

53

and Gerhard Mueller. Do folk think it a coincidence that their journey in 1887 took the route we followed? The only thing that puzzles me is why Charlie and Mueller took twenty years to get around to doing it. Go past the Haast River junction, I said, and head up the Clarke River, only don't get caught in the gorges. Well, Charlie and Mueller listened, so at the start of the gorges they made for the crest of the Solution Range, which offered useful vantage points for Mueller's survey work. Then they followed along the range until they could cut down the same slope that you followed down to the flat this evening. They did a compass traverse down the upper gorge of the Clarke, then returned to Docherty Pass, and eventually crossed the Solution Range to the Landsborough.'

'I reckon you're right, Bill. But I seem to recall Charlie in one of his notebooks giving a good description of what is now called Lower Otoko Pass, and saying that Gerhard Mueller was the first to climb it. How do we account for that?'

'You tell me. Haast was not much admired on the Coast, and neither did the Hokitika Survey Office have much regard for his map. Charlie and Mueller ignored him and forgot about me: that is as good as I can figure it.'

'Where exactly did you and Hassing get to, Bill, after climbing Docherty Pass? Hassing does seem confused, writing about a plateau with a lagoon in the middle of it, then heading down a creek and discovering your own campsite of a week earlier at its junction with a river. I've heard it argued that you must have gone down to the lake in the head of the Otoko Valley, then crossed Upper Otoko pass to the Landsborough. But it sounds to me like you probably wandered around on the Solution Range and then headed down Saddle Creek to the Clarke River. Could you clear the matter up?'

Bill looks a little embarrassed. 'I am sorry, I cannot. I'm dead, remember? It is you who are putting these words into my mouth. You can make the dead speak – that is your prerogative – but it is not within my powers to establish your nocturnal ramblings as historical fact. It is late and you are tired. Unless you could perhaps find a wee dram tucked away in the recesses of that swag, it would be best for me to move on.'

The moon was moving above the Solution Range, as if it too was making for Docherty Pass. Ice lay heavy on the grass and in the water, yet I felt snug in my sleeping bag, and the pain in my ankle had subsided to a tight persistent throb. I fell into deep sleep, undisturbed by past or present.

Dawn revealed everything white with frost: grass, earth, rock, sleeping bag. Somewhere above, among the cliffs, keas complained to each other about the cold; obviously they did not feel like stirring either. The stream ran sluggishly between iced up banks. Mist lay in the corners of the flat. The sun would still be a long time coming: it too had to climb over the Solution Range.

Being able to see the world generally makes it less intimidating, but even in full daylight Mt Hooker loomed large and menacing. I had come a long way to climb it: was I still determined to carry out the plan? It appears that I was not. Although in my warm sleeping bag I felt more or less equal to my surroundings, the idea of finding a route up 1500 metres of cold rock and ice made me tremble. It was easy to think of excuses. In particular, that right ankle was in a bad way; when I tried to stand on it I toppled headlong in the tussock. Nor did my lightweight boots inspire any confidence. But the simple fact was that I felt vulnerable and uncertain, and not at all in control of the situation. Since the weather did not look unsettled I could not use that as an excuse. No. Pain, cold and, most of all, the unfamiliarity of the landscape had cowed me; I had no inner resources left to cope with any additional danger or hardship. On edge, off balance, I simply wanted to get back to civilisation by the simplest route while the weather held and my ankle still functioned. Docherty Pass into the Otoko Valley beckoned.

So when the sun finally reached me and the frost began to smoke upon the grass, I packed up, crossed the stream, and hobbled along to the upper end of the flat, traversing firm ground that in daylight was as plain as day. Where the stream that descends from the pass enters the flat, I climbed the slope on its Mt Hooker side, then sidled slowly across frozen scrub and scree to reach the stream again where a large cairn beside a waterfall marks the route. My right ankle was not enjoying itself, particularly when sudden movement forced it take all the strain. However, from the cairn it was only a short climb up grassy slopes to the pass itself, and there a sheltered hollow just below the crest gave both my ankle and I the opportunity to rest and regain composure. Above, the long east ridge of Mt Hooker disappeared into the distance, rising in an endless sequence of rock steps and towers, while on the far side of the pass the East Hooker Glacier spilled down towards me with a sunny, almost welcoming appearance. The grass on which I sat was soft and green, with a few late gentians nodding in the slight breeze doing their best to cheer me up; and sitting there, with sunlight on my face and the makings of lunch spread on the grass around me, I did begin to feel braver again, a little more in control. It became possible to almost regret my decision not to attempt Mt Hooker, but I could not fool myself entirely.

From the pass there is no need to descend to the glacier, for the terrace that leads northward above it offers easy travel. It is the obvious way to go (no doubt Docherty and Hassing would also have followed this route), until bluffs make it necessary to climb a little to gain the ridge that descends into the Otoko Valley from the end of the Solution Range.

Although it is only 500 metres down to the valley floor, it took me a long time, for I was moving very slowly, trying to keep the weight off that ankle. Where I reached the flat there was a large rock beside a stream that offered shelter. There had to be other, more established dry rocks here at the head of the valley, I knew, but the fact that this one was close by outweighed other considerations, such as its low ceiling and a floor covered in birdshit and feathers. As I began to clear away some of the stones and ordure for sleeping room, a group of keas, obviously the proprietors, gathered on top of the rock next door to voice their disapproval. Their screeching stopped only while they ate the food scraps thrown their way as placatory gifts. Throughout the night they worked in shifts, complaining in injured tones of the rude manner of their eviction and the frost nipping their toes, until relieved by the next watch, which in turn did its best to ensure that I remained sleepless. When in the morning I emerged from under the rock they had bags under their eyes. Still, they had achieved their objective, for my night had also been far from restful, and, as well as feeling sore and vulnerable, I continued to feel a sense of trespass, of being misplaced and out of control. This made the idea of human shelter seem comforting, and since my map showed a hut at Reynolds Flat, further down the valley, that was where I decided to go.

Immediately below the old moraine, the alpine scrub and forest began, and I made heavy going of it. Although there was room to manoeuvre between the river and the valley walls, the terrain was tricky. The rocks were moss–covered and slippery, the side streams awkward to cross and the water cold. The rock walls lining the valley were steep and intimidating, and seemed to block out the sun for an unreasonable length of time. I pushed through windfalls and wrestled with thick fuchsia and mountain holly choking the stream beds. Unsure of whether to stay close to the river or above it, I wasted a lot of time and energy climbing up hillsides and terraces, then down again.

However, I did find traces of a deer trail, overgrown and blocked by windfalls. Following it required close concentration; at creek crossings it tended to disappear altogether, leaving me thrashing about in the undergrowth until I found it again. Yet it was well placed and intelligently graded; there could be little doubt that it was a major arterial route for animals that knew exactly where they were going, and that it linked with the well–defined route I had encountered rising out of the Landsborough Valley on the Solution Range. When I could follow it, it led steadily down the valley through beech forest and kamahi, winding across terraces, avoiding bluffs, and keeping a sensible distance above the river. When I did lose it at creek crossings, a careful search for it on re–entering the bush was effort well spent. Nor was I the first to benefit from the mountain sense of the deer: in one beech grove a solitary marker of red metal, and at other points old sprays of luminescent paint on tree trunks, showed that humans as well as animals had made good use of the trail in the past.

After several hours the trail emerged onto the small clearing of Stag Flat – grassy, sunny and pleasant, except for the remains of a shooters' camp festering at the bush edge. Big heavy relics indicated that this had been an airborne commercial operation rather than a recreational hunters' camp, and therefore part of the reason for the forlorn state of the deer trail.

Deer moved into South Westland during the 1920s and 1930s, following their release at Lake Kaniere to the north and Lake Hawea to the south. Particularly for those that crossed the Main Divide from Lake Hawea, the Landsborough Valley became an important migratory route. Long distance seasonal movement was common and valleys such as the Otoko, with their passes snow–free in summer, offered easy passage across the ranges. Countless hooves packed the earth and scarred the rocks, browsing mouths nibbled back the bush; networks of trails, local and arterial, clear and easy to follow for deer and humans alike, were established everywhere. Deer route–finding, of course, was based on familiarity with the landscape built up over many journeys, and passed on from one generation to the next. Until the 1970s, many a human explorer simply followed where the deer led, and so moved through the mountains with relative ease and certainty.

The venison boom of the 1960s and 1970s changed all that. It was a latter day gold rush; there were fortunes to be made and not all those involved took much notice of attempts at legal and bureaucratic regulation. Competition was fierce, the slaughter enormous. Helicopters fitted with sirens flew along the treeline to frighten the deer out of the forest onto the open tops, where shooters with automatic rifles were landed to mow them down. Then the hunters and deer carcasses were flown out again, the venison rushed to road–heads and prepared for export, the hunters to the next valley or mountainside to repeat their performance. Conflicts over poaching on the territory of others were common, sabotage and warning shots across the bows of men and choppers not unheard of, and the accident rate was high. By the 1980s the rush was over. Hunters and helicopters had multiplied, the deer had become far fewer and smarter; the traumatised survivors learned to run deeper into the forest when disturbed by men rather than up onto open hillsides, and to venture into the open only with extreme caution and preferably under the cover of darkness.

Decimation of the herds has meant that their trails, too, have gone into decline. While there is some local traffic by bush–dwelling deer, it is not enough for effective maintenance. Like the main Otoko trail, all the long–distance tracks are in serious disrepair, overgrown and difficult to follow. The bush has reverted to something like its state before the deer were released, which is good in environmental terms, but less so for weary travellers intent on finding their way home. Besides, I have never felt animosity towards the deer or found joy in their destruction; in fact, as an immigrant to the shores of Aotearoa, I have tended to identify with them.

From Stag Flat the deer trail climbed once more and sidled for a while, then headed towards the river, where, crossing the first big creek, I lost it again. And so the journey continued until late afternoon, when the valley opened out on the green grass of Reynolds Flat. A search of the bush edge again failed to turn up the hut shown on the map. (It had burned down some fourteen years earlier.) By now, however, I was becoming inured to this sort of disappointment. Gritting my teeth, I limped on. Although there was supposed to be an old horse track through the bush beside the river from the bottom of Reynolds Flat, I could not locate the start of that either. So I hobbled down the edge of the river until it became too dark to continue, then camped under a boulder beside the stream, just out of reach of the spray. Ice formed on the stones around me during the night.

Next morning it was less than an hour to where the river turns sharply and flows out of the bush onto open flats. When those flats, dotted with grazing cattle, came into view, I relaxed for the first time since leaving Barron Saddle. The river was so low that I could cross the main stream at will, aiming directly from one bend in the river to the next, taking the shortest and easiest route out to the highway. There I hitched a ride north to Franz Josef Glacier, where Alex and Suzy Miller made me welcome. No sooner had I stopped walking than my left knee swelled up tightly, in belated response at having to take over much of the work from my right ankle, and the spell of fine autumn weather gave way to a violent storm that lashed the coast and mountains with torrential rain for six days. It was not the sort of weather in which to be searching for non–existent huts in the Landsborough or the Otoko.

On the seventh day I set off back to the eastern side of the mountains via Copland Pass. Alex looked at my knee, shook his head, and offered to fly me back over the range in his aeroplane. But, no, I insisted that I was all right, that my difficulty in bending the knee was only a temporary thing, that it was on the mend. The familiar Copland Valley looked particularly uninviting as I started up it, with black cloud hanging down to the valley floor, lifting only briefly to reveal fresh snow right down into the forest. The Welcome Flat hut–site was a mess. Only three months earlier a landslide had swept down the valley wall above, demolishing the brand new hut, which now lay half–buried under a flow of mud and rock and broken trees. Fortunately nobody had been killed. In terms of my journey, however, it was just one more missing hut. The hot springs, which had been spared, still filled the cold air with their steam and sulphide smell. Tempting though it was to bathe my knee and ankle in hot water, I pushed on to Douglas Rock Hut. By the time I reached it, I was seriously regretting my refusal of Alex's offer.

The next day, despite a knee that could not bend and an ankle struggling to support me, I made it to the pass, where the weather held off long enough for a slow–motion dash over the top. Although the cloud was thick and snow laden, the rocks iced and the upper slopes dissected by crevasses, I could continue on my way confidently, if painfully, for here I knew the terrain well. In due course I emerged from the cloud at Hooker Hut. *That* was still there, at any rate (thanks to the efforts of Alex Miller, Bruce Jenkinson, Merv Burke and Phil Boswell, who, in 1963, moved it back from the edge of the moraine wall that was collapsing onto the Hooker Glacier). From the hut it was an even slower journey, in the dark, down to Mount Cook Village.

CHAPTER SIX

The Way gathers in emptiness;
emptiness is the fasting of the mind.
— Chuang Tzu, *Inner Chapters*

It was late in March 1989 that the bus dropped me off once more at the Paringa River Bridge. There was still the unfinished matter of Mt Hooker. The river flats near the highway were bright with the cool sunshine of autumn; Mt Hooker and the other mountains at the head of the Paringa and Otoko Rivers were invisible under dark cloud.

On the other side of the road, a party of hunters were organising themselves to fly into the Otoko. They were lavishly equipped and festooned with guns and knives, but very friendly. Tony Condon, who runs cattle in the Paringa–Otoko Valley and whose farmhouse is several hundred metres up the road, was helping with their preparations. When I told Tony that I planned to go up the Paringa River and over into the head of the Clarke to climb Mt Hooker, he offered to take me to his hut at the Paringa–Otoko junction by jet boat. He would be doing some shooting there overnight and I was welcome to join him and his friend.

It was an offer impossible to refuse. Soon James Scott arrived from Karangarua by helicopter to fly in the shooters. After they had gone, while waiting for Tony to finish his chores at home, I sorted out my own baggage, which seemed terribly heavy and bulky. In addition to the usual climbing and camping gear, there was enough food for two weeks, a tent (no more of those non–existent huts for me, thank you very much!), and a two–way mountain radio for emergency communication. This last had been requested by Janette: the anxieties aroused by my going off into the hills alone were bad enough, without the additional concern triggered by the previous episode regarding my body's ability to withstand the rigours of the journey. Carrying a radio seemed a sensible thing to do. This was the only journey on which I have carried either a tent or a radio, and in

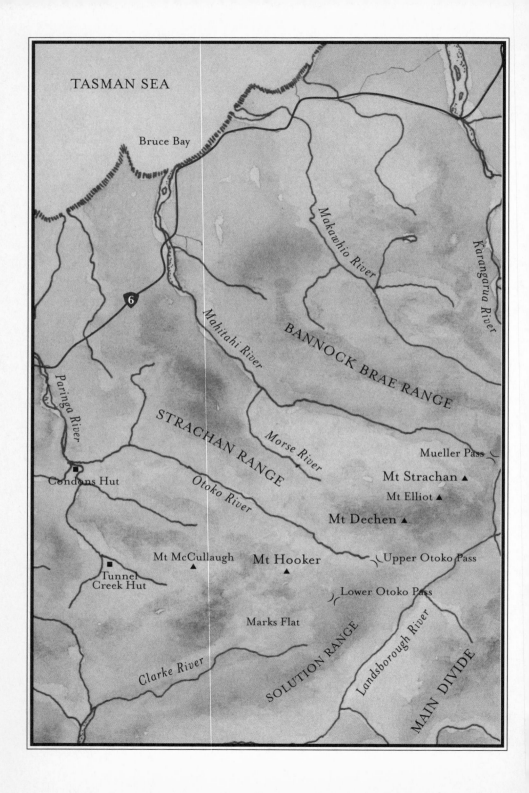

the event both turned out to have more than comfort value.

So there was plenty of luggage. More important, however, was the issue of mental baggage, for it was this that had weighed me down on the previous occasion. In many cultures there is a tradition of venturing into the mountains to purify the mind, to empty it of extraneous concerns and concentrate on what is essential. Sometimes this is expressed in terms of the healing properties of nature, which most of us believe we have experienced at some time or other when we return from the mountains or the sea refreshed, invigorated and with a sense that we can see things in proper perspective again. But there is a limit to what the natural world can do. If we go into the mountains preoccupied and weighed down by worries, it is likely that our distracted state, our inability to focus on the task at hand, will get us into trouble. So if stilling and cleansing the mind is our goal, it is a mistake to think that we can avoid the hard work this requires simply by removing ourselves to a wilderness setting, in the belief that the natural world will somehow do everything for us: quieting and ordering the confusion of unarticulated perceptions and inchoate ideas, the turmoil of emotion, feeling, desire, dread, ambition and frustration.

Being a hermit is a state of mind, not a matter of physical location. Detachment, equanimity, clarity: these qualities can be attained in society no less than in the mountains – and, indeed, take on greater value there. The fasting of the mind is not a discipline that can be left to moments of leisure.

On my previous journey I had been burdened with concerns I was unable to resolve. Certainly the heaviest of these had been the death, eighteen months earlier, of my infant daughter Aletta. While externally the mourning was over, internally it continued, with loss and hurt harrowing our family life and intensifying the stress of everyday concerns.

I had also been troubled by a change in career path. In general, I have found career paths harder to follow than tracks in the wilderness; their traces have always appeared faint at best, and just when I need a little reassurance to lead me through an uncertain stretch, the markers have a habit of disappearing altogether. Most of the time I feel I've been pushing through the undergrowth looking for a career path rather than actually following one. Certainly in 1987 it seemed that way. I had just moved from university life to a position in the government bureaucracy and was feeling disoriented and unsure of myself – in the midst of what might be called a chronic (as opposed to an acute) identity crisis.

Now, two years later, I was more composed, the world and I had become more attuned. Aletta was still with me, but the grief had softened and diffused, leaving me grateful for her memory rather than pained by her loss. Moreover, since the 1987 journey, Saskia had been born, filling Janette and I with the visceral joy and optimism of new life. If that made the career side of things seem trivial, a job change had nevertheless improved that too, enabling me to find more personal continuity and satisfaction in what I was doing. I was therefore in a much better state for entering the mountains: what might be called light headed.

On the way up river the gathering darkness was cold and cutting, carrying with it an edge of winter, but Tony's hut among the trees provided a welcome snugness. Company and a shared meal helped to generate a feeling of belonging that was to last throughout my journey, reinforcing my sense of harmony and easing the transition to solitude. I felt relaxed – at one with my surroundings.

The morning was heavy with moisture – an enormous sponge waiting to be to squeezed – grass and forest dripped with dew, while the cloud hung so near to the valley floor that it left only just enough space for the sound of the river to reach us. The rain had not yet begun, but it was close. Tony and his off–sider went out to locate the deer they had shot the previous evening, and place them where James Scott would be able to retrieve them later in the day. I shouldered my pack and set off up the Paringa.

The track wound around the edge of the clearing, then headed up the valley through mixed forest whose trunks were covered with kiekie and epiphytes. This track too was overgrown, and faint in places, but easy enough to follow thanks to white metal markers nailed to the trees; when it eluded me at creek crossings and big windfalls it was never for long. The forest floor was relatively open under the large trees, the valley wide and in no hurry to climb. Still the rain held off, the cloud base now a little higher than before. Scarcely a leaf stirred. Even with a heavy load it was comfortable going, for the need to remain watchful of the track's wanderings gave me an excuse, when I needed one, to move slowly.

Tunnel Creek Hut stood rusting on the river bank in a small clearing. The sun doing its best to break through was reason enough to rest for a while and eat. Noiselessly, the transparent river glided over its stones as I sat beside it studying the way ahead. This was where the hard work would begin. Just upstream of the hut, Tunnel Creek joined the river, and on its true left bank the route followed up a ridge to the treeline, then sidled to the right above the bush, to return to the infant Paringa River above the precipitous gorge through which it falls. The pass I was aiming for leads from the very beginning of the river to the McCullaugh Creek tributary of the Clarke River.

A doe and her fawn showed me the way across the river at Tunnel Creek, but were in no mood to guide me the rest of the way. The ridge began steeply, at first forcing me to climb on scrub growing up against the rock of the valley wall, treading gently lest it come unstuck. Soon it re-lented to become a steady ascent that quickly had me sweating heavily and my shoulders complaining under their load. White markers continued to appear periodically to assure me that I was still on course. Then it began to rain, lightly at first – a steady drizzle that drifted gently down through the foliage of the beech trees. I had entered the cloud; it was not that I had been climbing fast, but rather that the cloud had come down to meet me, with the obvious intention of keeping me company for some time to come.

Where the spur levelled off the rain grew heavier. My world shrank to a sodden patch of beech forest, bemisted and perforated by a hard cold rain. After following the ridge for a couple of kilometres and crossing a swampy hollow, the route climbed steeply again to reach the treeline a long way above the river. Although in the Tunnel Creek Hut book there had been mention of a comfortable bivouac rock here, I had not memorised the directions for finding it, so now passed a frustrating time searching for it in wet scrub. No luck. The directions were 1000 metres below me in the hut and evening was approaching, but I was carrying a tent, so I might as well use it. On I went, following a faint track around the hillside and across a stream, then climbing past a tarn to a rise overlooking the alcove of the upper Paringa River.

While the rain had stopped, dense cloud continued to drive in from the sea. The light was harsh and it was cold. One last time I crossed the small stream of the Paringa, then climbed beside it to the foot of the final slope to the pass, where I pitched my tent on a patch of stunted tussock and tutu as a violent wind hurled cloud against the hillside, and rain and darkness closed in about me.

In the uncertain and ambiguous light of morning, the northwest wind pushed me to the top of the pass. Reflecting on it now, it seems rather unlikely that the ridge–top was actually swaying in the gusts, but it seemed that way at the time. I certainly kept a firm grip on the rock as I moved across it. There was a brief glimpse of black walls rising into the mist on my left, while in front of me the cloud coiled over the drop into the McCullaugh basin and disappeared. The route was obvious, for countless deer hooves had carved a well–formed path down the rock slabs below the pass, veering to the right before descending to the tussock covered slopes of the basin. Grateful for the efforts of the deer, I followed their trail unheedfully. Too unheedfully, actually, for all too soon I had lost it among enormous tussocks whipped by the wind and lashed by the rain, and ended up slithering abruptly down to the creek. Then I made my way down beside it, as the rain became heavier, the morning darker. Side streams swelled, tussocks sprayed water and light as they writhed on the wind, earth and stones oozed downhill. The entire landscape was awash.

Just below the treeline the bottom fell out of McCullaugh Creek, sending it plummeting in bursts of foam and spray in the direction of the Clarke River. My own route was a little less direct. A deer trail led away left from the creek, climbing slightly as it rounded a spur and then dividing. Soon there were deer trails running off in all directions, demanding that I choose those most inclined to follow a leftward diagonal down to the river. In the forest there was no wind at all; everything was still and wet and green. From moss, ferns and leaves, greens light and dark dripped in the air around me, splashing soundlessly from branch to branch to wash on the verdant forest floor.

A trail led to a small rock shelter where the odour of deer was strong, fresh hoof prints in dry sand showing that its resident had left as I approached. Lower there was another, slightly larger overhang, also hurriedly vacated. Here I rested for a while, feeling rather guilty at the thought that somewhere not far away a vexed deer was peering with annoyance from the wet forest understorey, waiting for the uninvited guest to make himself scarce. On a day like today a fur coat would take a long time drying.

Rain, dripping trees, drenched lichens, moss swollen with water, and, in my wake, mud: the world had turned to slush and I was being washed downhill like alluvium. A descent of 1000 metres from the pass brought me to Monro Flat on the Clarke River, where the river was running high. On the opposite bank the clearing was still above water, but on my side the river was eating away at the forest edge. Another fifteen minutes splashing up the valley and I came to the Murdock Creek junction. From there, however, further progress was out of the question. Murdock Creek thundered down its rocky bed, its floodwaters sluicing boulders into the Clarke. To cross was impossible; and anyway, even were I to succeed, I would still have to ford the Clarke River itself just upstream, in order to gain access to the route through the gorge to Marks Flat. The only sensible thing to do was wait for the flood level to fall.

At the bush edge, on a level patch of moss bejewelled with purple and white coprosma berries, I pitched my tent, well pleased that I had brought it. Around mid–afternoon the cloud thinned for a while, allowing watery sunshine to filter through, drying me and my belongings. But all too soon I had to retreat to the tent, as once more the rain came down torrentially, relentlessly, filling the valley with a roar that merged with the thunder of the rivers – a din of water amplified by the mountain walls that hemmed me in. It continued throughout the night, unceasing. Then at dawn, long after I had given up hope for the day, it suddenly stopped, and a few hours later the sun was shining, drawing steam from rock and foliage alike. But Murdock Creek was still running higher than ever.

Sitting in the sun, listening to the river, I thought of Mueller and Douglas, who in 1887 descended the section of the Clarke River that I was now waiting to go up. They did a compass traverse down the gorge to this creek junction, and later, after their journey to the head of the Landsborough, completed their mapping task by returning to the lower reaches of the Clarke and following it up to Monro Flat. Mueller's thoroughness and enthusiasm as a surveyor commands admiration; his map of the Landsborough–Clarke basin was a great piece of work.

Early in the afternoon, to check conditions and get some exercise, I scrambled up beside Murdock Creek. Far above, the stream poured over a cliff on the valley wall, while higher still the mountains remained lost in cloud. Pottering along the bank of the torrent I had a pleasant surprise. A large tree, swept down by the flood, lay across the creek, bobbing on the current, its roots near my bank, its crown wedged among the boulders on the far side; it had branches enough along its trunk to provide safe passage even with a heavy pack. So with any luck I might still reach Marks Flat today after all.

I packed quickly, making for the crossing before the weather could change its mind. It was simple and I didn't even get my feet wet. This, however, was only the briefest of aberrations, for ten minutes later, crossing the waist–deep Clarke, they resumed the sodden state that is the normal condition of feet in Westland. Still, reaching the true left bank of the Clarke was much easier than I had any right to expect after the rain that had fallen; perhaps the precipitation higher up had not been as heavy as down in the valley.

The climbing began abruptly. A quick rise led to a crest a hundred metres above the river, where a pool of black water lay dark in shadow and stillness, then up onto the rocky hillside above the gorge. The slow work was made easier by a deer trail. Only when I doubted the deer's judgement and accused them of climbing too high above the river did I get myself into trouble. I should have remembered that deer do not exert themselves unnecessarily, and simply accepted the fact that I was the new boy here.

As it climbed, the trail passed a number of small overhangs, some quite spacious, and, obviously, all of them vacated by deer. It occurred to me that I might unintentionally be mustering a herd of resentful stags and fretful does with frightened fawns running at their heels. What if they should turn and make a stand? But the rain held off, there were bursts of sunshine, and I encountered no deer, so perhaps they were not so fussed by my intrusion after all.

I climbed very slowly, with the gorge below visible through the beech trees. Soon there was another overhang, this one large enough to accommodate a weary tramper. However, I still wanted to reach Marks Flat while the weather held. At the front of the sheltered floor of the overhang I stepped up onto a low parapet of rock, to get around the wall beyond. Not watching what I was doing, I put my left foot in a crack in the rock; the boot jammed tight, then pushed me off balance. I struggled to stay upright, but to no avail; in slow–motion I tipped outward, in the direction of the gorge, while at the same time the weight of my pack pulled me backwards. As soon as I was out of plumb, the pack exerted its full force and a few seconds later I was half hanging, half lying upside down, suspended by my left foot, the pack doing its best to stretch my frame and prevent me from returning to an upright position in the foreseeable future. With my head pointing in the direction of the gorge and the roar of its waters, the river suddenly seemed far too close for comfort.

CHAPTER SEVEN

A continued gravity keeps the spirit too much bent;
we must refresh it sometimes, as we bait in a journey
that we may go on with greater ease.
– John Dryden, *An Essay of Dramatic Poesy*

Now that is not a sight one sees often. Let us just leave me hanging there for a while, by my left boot, since I am in no great danger and feeling more foolish than frightened. It is not likely that my foot will suddenly come free and precipitate me down the side of the gorge and into the river. True, were I careless in freeing myself, I could damage my knee or break my leg, which would be a problem; or I could lose the heavy pack that is hanging from my shoulders, and it would certainly be difficult to get back to civilisation were *it* to disappear into the river.

While I am hanging here trying to remember which way is up, as pack, ice–axe and the contents of my pockets do their best to obey gravity, it will be convenient to remove some of the mental baggage I have been carrying, to get rid of some of the rocks in my head and lighten the load. So stand over me and command: 'Confess your errors, delusions, half–baked ambitions, all those things that you hoped you could get away with because there was no one about at the time to witness their effects, yet which continue to weigh you down. Confess or we'll undo your bootlace and let gravity have her way with you.'

Gravity is a problem for mountaineers and explorers. Many find it hard to laugh at themselves or reflect on the preposterousness of their actions, the absurdity of the situations into which they get themselves. Some develop egos that envelop entire mountain ranges, ice–caps, oceans, river systems. Instead of emptying their minds in order to respond alertly to the environment, they project their egos onto it and reduce the world to a setting for their triumphs, a setting in which success is just a matter of determination or strength of will, a question of wanting to succeed badly enough. Wish and reality blur, and disaster follows. As ambition or desire takes hold, it becomes difficult to respond flexibly when events unfold in ways other than those anticipated or planned. The idea has become an obsession that grips the mind; eyes turn inward, no longer capable of focusing on what is actually happening.

Ambition requires imagination, a capacity to entertain bold conceptions and understand what is required to realise them. On the other hand, realism or caution calls for imagination too: the ability to conceive what could go wrong. Coming to grief through 'unforeseen circumstances' is tantamount to death from lack of imagination.

I have read of heroes who say they are blessed with a lack of imagination and so do not exhaust themselves wrestling with dangers and difficulties that may not materialise. That is not a category to which I belong; I have always been amply endowed with imagination, expending a lot of energy in processing all the what–ifs and losing many a night's sleep coping with crises that never eventuate. But it is important to be able to prefigure the worst possible scenarios as well as the best – indeed more important as far as staying alive is concerned.

Still, an over–active imagination sometimes creates its own problems. When I was eighteen years old, and had lived in New Zealand only a few months, I set off on my first solo mountaineering excursion. In cloud and drizzle I climbed up somewhere to the right of the Otira Face of Mt Rolleston, near Arthurs Pass, crossing to the head of the Waimakariri River. Fortunately nothing went wrong, despite my limited experience, and the following day I made my way down to Carrington Hut, in the beech forest near White River junction. That night a southwest wind roared through the trees, whose branches swayed and groaned in the bright moonlight and scratched against the corrugated iron walls of the hut. There was only me and my imagination there, I knew, but I was scared. Outside the scratching was erratic, loud, unpredictable; inside the shadows from my candle reared and leapt upon the walls. There was no one there to laugh at me, so I snuffed out the candle, crawled into my sleeping bag, zipped it up tight over my head and shut my eyes. I was safe!

It was not a likely beginning for a career of solo heroics in the mountains. And while unburdening myself of memories that make my cheeks burn, I have to confess also the time I was splashing my way down a narrow, winding gorge. It was a hot day, the water was deep, and I wanted to keep my clothes dry, so was wearing boots and nothing more. As I rounded a corner I startled a party of fishermen, and their wives even more. Modern man finds it hard to claim to be 'clothed in virtue', as medieval Christian commentators liked to explain away nudity in classical literature, so all I could do was try to maintain a composed and dignified countenance until around the next bend. To their credit, the fisherpersons managed to control their laughter until I was out of earshot.

It is becoming harder and harder for me to read accounts of expeditions and autobiographies of famous explorers and climbers. I am increasingly repulsed by the risk–taking, the near misses and fatalities, the sheer unpleasantness of it all. The accounts portray personalities that appear as selfish as they are humourless, and often the reader is given to understand that total self–absorption, egotism, ruthlessness, single–minded competitiveness and a refusal to be distracted or deterred by anything from the task at hand are the basis of success. It has become commonplace for climbers on Everest and K2 to step over the bodies of dead predecessors. Sometimes members of one expedition refuse to help those from another in trouble because it may lessen their own chances of achieving their goal.

It appears that in 1996 on the north ridge of Everest a pair of climbers making their way to the summit moved past three others who lay dying in the snow, without making any attempt to help them. They subsequently defended this disregard by saying that they did not know the men who were dying and that 8000 metres above sea level is no place for morality. It is an argument that has been made more generally. In extreme circumstances, such as a famine or natural disaster, it is claimed that conventional morality does not apply, that the ordinary rules of concern and compassion break down. It becomes a case of lifeboat ethics in which the overriding concern of each individual becomes personal survival.

The argument inverts historical experience. If the rules of conventional morality do not apply in extreme situations, it is because, when the margin for survival is narrow, morality demands *more,* not less. Amongst peoples who dwell in hostile environments, rules for providing support and hospitality, even to strangers, are usually strict. At sea, in warfare, in mountain search and rescue, heroism in order to help or save others is treated as commonplace and habitual; it is what is normal and expected. Although it is understood that not everyone is able to set aside fear and self–interest in extreme circumstances, we respect those who do so precisely because they remain true to their essential humanity. There are those who have the strength to remain socially alert and morally responsible to the point of death.

Merely because some or even most of us fail in this regard does not mean that the basic principles are irrelevant. In the case of Himalayan climbers, who put themselves in extreme situations by choice, the plea that they have moved beyond the rules of normal morality is particularly odious. It seeks to legitimate ignoring the needs of others because a self–imposed task demands it. History is littered with those who have regarded their causes as so momentous that they have felt able to transcend the rules governing ordinary mortals. This argument is specious at the best of times, but to find it made in regard to the frivolous activity of mountaineering is absurd, an attempt at self–justification by individuals who cannot face up to the fact of their own mediocrity. The ability to cope with hardship or travel through hostile terrain is not proof of intrinsic superiority after all.

The lack of good sense, humour and fundamental humanity that troubles such expeditions is also evident in the sensationalised accounts of them, the way they glorify disaster and work every nasty situation for the last gasp of excitement. To impress the public and to sell books, the authors celebrate the close shaves and disasters, while glossing over the errors of judgement that caused them. We are impressed by those who endure hardship and triumph over adversity, yet such triumphs appear hollow when we learn that the suffering was unnecessary, a consequence of ignorance, error and inability or refusal to learn from one's own mistakes or those of others.

The British Antarctic explorers of the early twentieth century are outstanding for their inability to learn from experience, the unnecessary hardship and suffering they endured as a result, and the manner in which their mistakes and failures were glorified by the public and their successors alike. Scott was an incompetent leader whose lack of judgement and inability to plan on his final attempt to reach the South Pole in 1911–12 caused his own death and that of his companions. Despite first hand experience in 1902–03 of the debilitating strain and perilous slowness of manhauling heavy sledges on foot, Scott never made any serious attempt to learn to ski or to handle dog teams. Although on his earlier expeditions he had first hand experience of scurvy, he failed even to identify the problem, let alone think how rations might be improved to overcome it. His supplies were inadequate, with no margin for error or delay, and his method of establishing supply depots was absurdly casual. On reaching the Polar Plateau, he increased the size of his party for the final push to the Pole, though all the preparations up to that point, in terms of equipment and supplies, had been made for a smaller party. Self–deluding to the end, he attributed his failure to bad luck in encountering bad weather and snow conditions that could not have been foreseen, when in reality they were much the same as he and Shackleton had encountered on earlier expeditions; and on many days when he considered conditions too awful to break camp, not that far away, in similar conditions, Amundsen and his men continued on their way to the Pole.

If Scott was the erratic autocrat, Amundsen was the complete professional. He was meticulous in his planning and preparation, and left nothing to chance. Unlike Scott, he understood the importance of social cohesion and knew how to get the best from his companions. His men were expert skiers, dog handlers and navigators; they had the intelligence and flexibility, as well as the experience, to continue refining their equipment until the last moment, even though it had been obtained from leading manufacturers. Their food supplies were plentiful, their depots far in excess of likely needs, and Amundsen, alert to the danger of scurvy, drew on his earlier Arctic and Antarctic experience to devise ways to combat it.

Above all, Amundsen had the humility and alertness necessary to learn from others. During his journey through the Northwest Passage in 1903–06, he learned all he could from the Inuit, the undisputed experts in survival and travel in polar regions. Under their tutelage he acquired the knowledge needed to be in control in their extreme environment, including which furs to wear for warmth and comfort, the importance of fresh meat for maintaining health and stamina, how to build igloos and, above all, how to care for dogs, handle them and drive sledges in all conditions.

Small details reveal huge differences. Where Scott's party marked their supply depots with a single cairn of snow and simply hoped they would be able to find them in storm or whiteout conditions, Amundsen used an elaborate system of markers set at right angles to his line of travel, extending as far as five kilometres on either side in the case of particularly important depots, with the markers no more than a hundred skiing paces apart, and each one recording the distance to the depot and whether it lay to the left or to the right. Scott's party found sledge hauling in very cold snow conditions nearly impossible; the snow was like sand, on which the sledge runners refused to slide; for exhausted men it was demoralising as well as debilitating. Amundsen had learnt from the Eskimo that in such conditions the appropriate technique is to apply a series of thin layers of ice to the soles of the runners, that iced runners glide easily and that layering the ice makes it elastic and prevents it from shattering.

It is not surprising, then, that Amundsen's account of his expedition to the South Pole seems casual and understated, even boring at times. For here was a group who knew precisely what they had to do and carried out their task to perfection; they were so thorough that they encountered nothing 'unforeseen' and had no really close shaves, despite pioneering a new route onto the Polar Plateau that was every bit as difficult as the route up the Beardmore Glacier first taken by Shackleton and followed by Scott.

Scott's accounts have come to epitomise what the public expects of expedition writing: high drama, misery and suffering, and if not death then at least plenty of risk–taking and stoicism evoked with emotion and gusto. It all makes for a good read, but appears admirable only if we avoid thinking about the reality. It is Amundsen rather than Scott who is admirable, and he is admirable precisely because, in a sense, he has so little to report. In his case everything went well, as he took care that it should.

And Shackleton? Over time his reputation has grown, and deservedly so. Shackleton's understanding of human needs and foibles, his sociability and sympathy, made him an effective leader. Although it failed to do what it set out to do, his *Endurance* expedition of 1914–16 was still a remarkable achievement: the entire party returned safely after their ship had been trapped in pack ice for nine months and had eventually sunk. Following a desperate voyage to Elephant Island, where most of the party remained, Shackleton and five others navigated the Antarctic Ocean in an open whaleboat to reach South Georgia Island and launch a rescue mission.

Nonetheless, Shackleton shared some characteristics with Scott, the colleague and arch–rival he despised. In particular, Shackleton was not good at learning from experience; his errors were habitual, manifestations of a personality he could not change. On his expedition of 1909, he came within 156 kilometres of the Pole; had he and his companions been competent skiers they would have reached their destination, despite not having dog teams to pull their sledges. Yet subsequently Shackleton neither took the trouble to master skiing himself nor ensured that his men were competent skiers. Although Amundsen (with the memory of his polar triumph fresh in his mind) persuaded Shackleton to take dogs along on the *Endurance* expedition for the ambitious plan of crossing from one side of Antarctica to the other, Shackleton took no one who was skilled in dog handling and driving. It would never have occurred to him to go and learn from the Inuit as Amundsen had done. Yet this did not inhibit him from making optimistic estimates of the daily distance he would travel on his crossing of Antarctica, a distance almost as great as Amundsen himself had managed to average. Such inflated self–belief would surely have been his undoing.

Having survived unscathed entrapment in the Weddell Sea ice floes, shipwreck, the ocean voyage by open boat and the crossing of South Georgia, and accomplished the rescue of the Elephant Island castaways, Shackleton concluded that Providence had watched over his party from the beginning. Well, that is as maybe. But if we accept this conclusion, then surely the most convincing evidence of the divine protection they enjoyed is the fact that Providence trapped their ship in the ice in the first place, and so prevented them from setting foot on the Antarctic continent. For it would have been obvious to an omniscient being that the Crossing party was going to its death, its personnel having learnt so little from the death and privation suffered by previous expeditions.

To criticise Scott or Shackleton simply for making mistakes would be absurd and unfair. Everyone makes mistakes, even an Amundsen. What makes Amundsen so impressive is the frankness he showed in facing up to his mistakes and the intelligence with which he worked to minimise them. Above all, for Amundsen self–inflicted danger and hardship were not reasons to swagger and strut in the public gaze; on the contrary, error was evidence that his mastery was incomplete, that there were more skills to be learned, deeper knowledge to be acquired. If public acclaim was to be won it was by evidence of complete control, apparent effortlessness, smooth progress, success and a safe return.

Dawn above the ridge leading to Eagle Peak, Mt Thomson and Mt Sefton, with the Mueller Valley under cloud and Aoraki/Mt Cook behind. (Photo: Craig Potton)

Being able to move in the mountains deftly, lightly, with a minimum of damage to oneself and to the environment, requires much more than skill at moving over rock and ice; it requires knowledge that can only be acquired gradually by being in the mountain setting and learning to read and respond to its signs. It includes knowledge of the way that mountain ridges shape air currents, and the feel of the air before rain; the impact of global warming on glaciers, and the impact of avalanches on people; how the lie of rock strata and a million years of water flow shape gorges and valley walls, and how an overnight flood can change them entirely; the effect of wind and winter shadow on forest, and how some types of lichen become slippery when wet; and an understanding of wildlife, or what is left of it. It is knowledge that entails an appreciation of the fact that what occurs below the snowline is just as significant as what occurs beyond it, that each illuminates the other.

ABOVE: Looking down the Douglas Valley from the western slopes of Maunga Ma. (Photo: Aat Vervoorn) LEFT: Upper Landsborough Valley and Mt Burns from the slopes of Fettes Peak. (Photo: Geoff Spearpoint)

In the process of turning dreams and plans into reality it is impossible to remain free of preconceptions; after all, preconceptions are precisely what imagination and mental preparation entail. What is necessary is to keep a rein on dreams and be able to revise plans in light of the weather, conditions, fitness, or overly optimistic assessments of our own abilities. This is easier to do when travelling alone than with others. It brings to mind the Daoist concept of non-action. 'Do nothing and there is nothing that is not done', says Laozi. He means that if we come with fixed ideas and preconceptions, and try to impose our will on events, we are likely to fail. Action succeeds when it is, in a sense, non-action, when our acts are entirely in accord with the disposition of things, so that it's as if our desired outcomes just happen by themselves. Successful action depends on correctly perceiving the innate tendency of situations (what does 'the innate tendency of situations' mean?) and understanding the importance of timing. This requires full alertness to what is going on around us and within us.

ABOVE: Tunnel Creek Hut, Paringa Valley. (Photo: Aat Vervoorn) LEFT: Forest interior, South Westland. (Photo: Aat Vervoorn)

Within a hundred metres of the road I had entered another world, one in which there existed only shades and textures of green: soft, pliant, still, alive, powerful. The forest canopy shut out noise and movement, washing in deeper green the ferns and lichens, the moss that covered tree-trunks and earth alike. On that moss I stepped without a sound, leaving no trace, as if treading on green light rather than the ground. Not even water broke the silence.

Bannock Brae Range from the Mahitahi Valley. (Photo: Aat Vervoorn)

Across the upper Mahitahi the peaks of the Bannock Brae Range, still deep in spring snow, jabbed at the sky, sharp overlapping plates of rock set on edge and exposed to the elements.

Looking across the head of Zora Creek, Landsborough Valley, toward the Main Divide. (Photo: Aat Vervoorn)

The soft snow, knee–deep, made progress slow. Soon consciousness narrowed until nothing remained other than the next step to be taken and the texture and pattern of the snow, its whiteness passing gradually beneath me, crystalline and heavy with water, its luminosity changing as swirls of cloud extended and retreated overhead. I rested frequently, turning to reflect on the line of footprints rising from far below, in a winding curve, to the purple plastic boots that kept me secure on the mushy surface. Time and sound ceased to exist; there was only snow and sunshine unfolding without end.

ABOVE: Aerial view looking toward the western aspects of Mt Sefton, Mt Thomson and Eagle Peak (at the far right of the skyline ridge). (Photo: Craig Potton) LEFT: Mt Hooker from Marks Flat. (Photo: Aat Vervoorn)

The immensity of the landscape unfolded as I climbed towards the summit of Mt Strachan. At my feet the ice of the Strachan Glacier spilled down into the Zora Valley, whose rock walls led down to the Landsborough River, while beyond the Landsborough, in a row, stood the mountains of the Main Divide. To the north lay the ranges of Westland, one after another, snowbound and uncompromising. The northeast was dominated by Mt Sefton and the cliffs of the Douglas Neve below it, with Eagle Peak also visible and looking grander than I remembered it. Above everything, however, rose the navigator peaks: Mt Tasman and Mt Dampier, and higher still the bulk and power of Mt Cook, intimidating even from a distance of thirty kilometres. Everything was silent, bathed in the light and clarity of morning, a stupendous world that would continue forever to reshape itself through the convection of molten rock, the power of water, the passage of wind and time.

ABOVE: Icefall, Mt Hooker. (Photo: Aat Vervoorn) LEFT: Aerial view of Mt Hooker from the west. (Photo: Craig Potton)

So off the ridge and into the ice debris I went. It was as if the glacier lacked the strength to hold itself together and was falling apart. Turning uphill again, I could jump from one ice hummock to the next, crampon around the weathered walls of seracs, and bridge my way out of crevasses. I was enjoying myself; it was a real life game of snakes and ladders. Near the head of the ice-fall a line of high seracs glistened blue and white in the fickle sunshine. Was this another dead end? Not at all. The ice gully up which I was walking led to a cleft between two imposing ice towers, from where the rear of the right hand tower revealed itself to be no more than an easy snow slope, sheltered from the weather by the shadow of its vertical neighbour. I could not literally walk up with my hands in my pockets, but almost. And there, stretching unbroken in front of me, was the smooth neve of the glacier, merging not far away with mist and cloud.

ABOVE: Author at bivvy site near Mt Du Fresne. (Photo: Aat Vervoorn) LEFT: Mt Du Fresne, with summit of Mt Tasman beyond. (Photo: Aat Vervoorn)

Overhead the sky was full of stars. The radiant edge of the galaxy spanned the valley, bridging with star clusters and constellations the space between one range and the other. Light that had been travelling for hundreds of millions of years fell around me like fine rain.

Evening light on the ridge climbed by author, with Big Mac in the foreground and Katies Col leading to Mt Torres and the summit of Mt Tasman. (Photo: Craig Potton)

Ranges grow and clouds gather, rocks break and rivers carry the silt to the sea. Mountains are processes, not fixed entities, yet in their slow change there is time enough for us to wonder and do some of what we dream. Moments come when all the elements converge, when mental clarity and stillness come together with physical fitness, when conditions in the mountains are favourable and the wind blowing from the right direction prompts us to venture out confidently.

Author on Fox Glacier neve, with Mt Tasman and Mt Torres behind. (Photo: Aat Vervoorn)

For years I had been biding my time, storing in my mind the idea of climbing the full west ridge of Mt Tasman, from the coastal plain to its summit on the Main Divide. In a single journey I would encompass all the zones of vegetation and alpine terrain that Westland compresses in its abrupt rise from the sea to permanent ice. Starting at 160 metres above sea level, at the edge of the Fox River flats, the ridge ends eighteen kilometres later on Mt Tasman's ice-cap at an altitude of 3497 metres. In straightforward terms this makes it the longest climb possible in New Zealand.

Sunrise on the eastern faces of Aoraki/Mt Cook and Mt Tasman, with the three peaks of Mt Haast in the foreground. (Photo: Craig Potton)

Steadily, slowly, we climbed, one foot, one hand at a time, ice-axes and crampons biting firmly into the frozen slope, now tending right, now tending left in order to relieve straining muscles. Our minds focused only on each successive move, nothing more, trying to ignore discomfort, not thinking about how much further or what lay ahead. Our torches cast only small circles of light on the snow in front of our faces; now and again little swirls of spindrift spun through the beams. The night was still except for the scratching of metal against ice and the sound of our breathing.

At our backs the sky began to lighten, spreading pale blue then red from the horizon and washing out the stars. Snow and ice soaked up colour, and daylight revealed the immensity of the mountain we were climbing. Wrinkles in the ice, rocks jutting out of the slope above, took a long time to reach and pass, while below the world unfolded, range after range taking shape above an ocean of cloud.

Take me now, still suspended by my left foot above the Clarke River. There is nothing very glorious about that; in fact, it is pretty silly. A moment of carelessness may lead to disaster, and when disaster strikes it avails little to tell yourself that you would have survived but for hunger, exhaustion, or the sweat running in your eyes. At such times the discovery that you have courage, or even greatness of soul and an unequalled capacity for suffering, are of little consolation. Errors of judgement are just as likely to have serious consequences as moments of carelessness, but they at least can be greatly reduced by a willingness to absorb the lessons of past experience. That is why my ascent of Eagle Peak was not an exemplary achievement: persevering in conditions that I knew to be dangerous is not something of which to be proud.

There have been other ignominious errors. I confess to my embarrassment the occasion I came out via Barron Saddle, tired and with food running low, after a week in the Douglas and the Landsborough. Instead of going back to Mt Cook Village via the moraines of the Mueller Glacier, I traversed high around the flank of Mt Darby to Sladden Saddle, and there ran out of steam completely. All I had left to eat was a packet of prunes. The dangers were obvious, but my body craved nourishment and I was too weak to resist. Incontinence makes it difficult to feel heroic. Fortunately it was a windless day, so I could take my pants off and wander across the snowfields bare–buttocked. Fortunately, too, it was late summer, so there was no one around to accuse me of indecent exposure, and I was able to slip out of Mt Cook National Park without being detected by rangers or made to clean up behind me.

On another occasion, when following an overgrown deer trail through thick forest in the Mahitahi Valley, I was using my ice–axe to brush away the veils of lichen hanging in the undergrowth, pushing it gently ahead of me to clear a path. Suddenly lichens that had been giving no more resistance than cobwebs changed their tack: absorbing the gentle force of the ice–axe, they fired it back at my forehead as if from a catapult; and there it embedded itself, the adze making a deep cut. Not paying much attention, I had failed to notice the strand of bush lawyer vine around which the lichen had been growing. A week later, when I turned up at the Millers' place at Franz Josef, Suzie observed the wound and commented dryly, 'Had it been the pick instead of the adze, the coroner would have had a difficult case on his hands.' Whether due to a gross error of judgement or casual carelessness, the fact that I would have formed a small category with Trotsky would have been no consolation at all.

Some errors are less embarrassing and sometimes it is difficult to judge whether a decision was actually an error or not. There are occasions when we go into something with our eyes open, see that events are not unfolding as they should, and manage to recover the situation in a controlled way that leaves us satisfied.

Consider an attempt I made to climb Mt Cook after not having been up it for many years. A couple of weeks in the mountains on the west of the Divide had made me fit, and the autumn weather was fine. There was only a slight chance of success, I knew, but I had three days to spare and it was worth trying. If it proved possible to get up through the ice–fall to the head of the Hooker Valley, with a little luck I would be able to climb the peak and return in the time available. True, mid–autumn is not a good time for going up the Hooker Valley, for the main ice–fall below Gardiner Hut is a tricky place at the best of times and even in early summer it may be impassable. Here the glacier rises more than 300 metres in one kilometre and the volume of ice travelling down the valley makes the ice–fall treacherous and chaotic. Some of its crevasses could easily swallow the family house, occupants and all, never mind a solitary traveller. In autumn those crevasses are at their gaping best, dark and bottomless, and the glacier ice is bare of snow, hard and slippery from the frosts. Still, over the years I have spent quite some time in the Hooker Ice–fall and have got to know its peculiarities well, so I had an idea of what I was letting myself in for.

By the time I set off from the village it was well into the afternoon. Evening shadows were deepening as I made my way past Hooker Hut, out towards the centre of the moraine covered glacier. In twilight I moved slowly over the loose boulders and gravel, trying to conserve energy for what lay ahead. The last glimmers of daylight enabled me to follow up the edge of the medial moraine, keeping off the white ice beside me in order to delay putting on crampons, but still benefiting from the light it reflected. When I reached the foot of the ice–fall it was already pitch dark.

Crampons fitted, torch on, I started up the steepening ice, its surface so hard that the crampon points scarcely marked it. Soon the crevasses started, first small, then bigger, the ice ridges separating them sharp and angular after the long summer melt. It demanded total concentration. No time for carelessness here. Slowly, painstakingly, I scrabbled upwards, around and through crevasses, under and over creaking ice blocks, crampon points scratching nervously on the polished surface, eventually working my way to the right, where a hollow in the glacier's surface usually gives access to the rock wall below Gardiner Hut.

The last crevasse before the rocks stopped me. The beam of my torch failed to reach the other side of the chasm separating me from the ice slope beyond, but I knew that even were I somehow to cross it, I would still have to get off the glacier onto the rock. Given the conditions confronting me, this no longer seemed plausible. Starlight glittered on the ice around me; a night wind eddied coldly amongst the pinnacles and arches, carrying with it the roar of water falling from ice–falls on the mountain wall above. It felt very hostile.

Carefully, precisely, I retraced my steps, feet sore from crampons that could not penetrate the ice, hands cold and bleeding from ice splinters and rocks embedded in crevasse walls. I had been tired from the effort of concentration; turning back redoubled that tiredness. Pinnacle followed pinnacle, crevasse followed unjumpable crevasse. In the blackness of night the ice–fall seemed endless. Now and again tiny scratch marks on the surface of the ice reassured me that I was keeping to my upward route, but most of the time the unmarked ice showed it had been indifferent to my passing. And time, like me, passed slowly. I knew I had to pace myself, taking each obstacle as it came, one by one, concentrating, not worrying about what might be around the next corner.

Eventually the ice–fall did end, but unfortunately the moraine–covered ice below it seemed no easier. I staggered over the rocks and tripped in the shadows cast by my torch. I was extremely tired now. In front of me the southern sky began to shimmer and blaze in sheets of yellow–green light; it flared, flashed, convulsed. Was my brain shortcircuiting from weariness? When I stopped to rest, leaning against a boulder, the lights continued to dance across the darkness. It was the aurora, translating the immensity of the cosmos into colours perceptible to human eyes. Yet not even for that magnificence could I keep my eyes open any longer. Steeling myself for one final push, I stumbled across to the edge of the glacier, lurched up the moraine wall, dropped my pack amongst the snow tussocks, and fell down asleep beside it. The stars winked at one another, but Aoraki's great silhouette said nothing. It did not have to.

Schemes always start in the imagination: something within us prompts the yearning to go and see for ourselves, to experience the unfamiliar. It may be a photograph, a book, or a traveller's tale told by the boring old man up the road, who amid an avalanche of words utters one phrase that triggers the mysterious process. I have always been fascinated by maps. By the age of five I had memorised all the countries of Europe, their shapes, colours and capitals, from an old German atlas that my father had acquired somewhere or other. I spend hours gazing at maps, trying to internalise the information recorded there, imagining what the terrain those marks represent on paper might be like in reality. It is a pity that poring over maps is not a perfect preparation for travelling through new country. Sometimes the act of looking down on the map is incorporated into the imagined landscape, so that it comes as a surprise to have to look *up* at the mountains. Or rain may be completely unexpected: 'There was no rain marked on my map, and in that photograph I saw the sky was unambiguously and unmistakably blue.' On a map, too, it is easy to draw a proposed route in straight lines, no matter how many contour lines and rivers they bisect. Euclid, who believed that the shortest distance between two points is a straight line, appears never to have lived in South Westland.

In the process of turning dreams and plans into reality it is impossible to remain free of preconceptions; after all, preconceptions are precisely what imagination and mental preparation entail. What is necessary is to keep a rein on dreams and be able to revise plans in light of the weather, conditions, fitness, or overly optimistic assessments of our own abilities. This is easier to do when travelling alone than with others. It brings to mind the Taoist concept of non–action. 'Do nothing and there is nothing that is not done', says Lao Tzu. He means that if we come with fixed ideas and preconceptions, and try to impose our will on events, we are likely to fail. Action succeeds when it is, in a sense, non–action, when our acts are entirely in accord with the disposition of things, so that it's as if our desired outcomes just happen by themselves. Successful action depends on an ability to perceive the tendencies unfolding within situations and understand the importance of timing. This requires full alertness to what is going on around us and within us.

Revising plans, scaling down dreams, cancelling aspirations altogether: these things usually give me little difficulty. At one time or another I have non–climbed most of the mountains in South Westland, many of them by a number of routes and in impressive combinations, as well as non–traversing numerous river gorges, glaciers and forests. This is not quite non–action in Lao Tzu's meaning, perhaps, but certainly in the sense of waiting for the right time, the moment will happen as if of its own accord. The problem is that in regard to most of those projects I am still waiting for the right time.

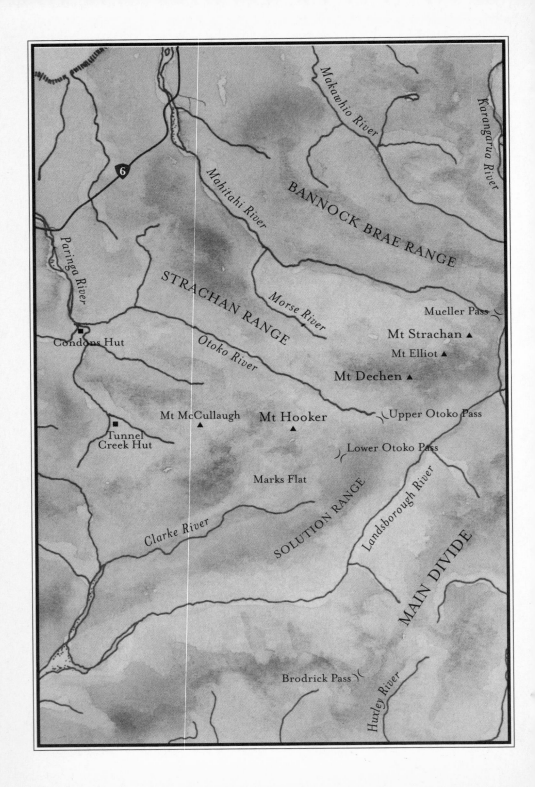

CHAPTER EIGHT

The learned Bishop Hall ... tells us ... "That it is an abominable thing for a man to commend himself;"–and I really think it is so.

And yet, on the other hand, when a thing is executed in a masterly fashion, which thing is not likely to be found out;–I think it is full as abominable, that a man should lose the honour of it, and go out of the world with the conceit of it rotting in his head.

    – Laurence Sterne, *The Life and Opinions of Tristram Shandy*

Eventually, still upside down, I managed to free first my left shoulder and then the right from the pack straps, while working the pack itself into a position from which it would be unlikely to make a dash for the river below. Then I worked my upper body (now lower, of course) into a horizontal position. From there, by clutching at holds in the rock with my right hand, I could raise head and shoulders further, until it was possible to hook my fingers over the upper edge of the rock, give a desperate heave and, by a manoeuvre approximating levitation, raise my backside to the same level. With my body realigned, extracting my foot from the crack was easy. It was a chastening experience.

As I continued climbing, the gorge narrowed and its sides became steeper. The deer trail turned up a scree slope that descended from the cliffs above right down into the gorge. After several minutes scrabbling up loose rocks, I began to mistrust the deer again and struck off on my own, moving off the scree into the scrub on its far side. Immediately I regretted it: they were right, *again*. After a struggle with unruly scrub and rocks, I relocated the trail where it descended after having avoided the obstacles, making its way down the river's edge at the beginning of the gorge.

Daylight was failing but I was unconcerned. Now it was just a matter of following up beside the river, past some big boulders and patches of scrub, to where a large cairn on top of the bivouac rock signalled welcome in the twilight. The rawness of the evening made me glad to crawl inside the shelter, get into my sleeping bag, and lie there simply enjoying the warmth while dinner cooked on the stove.

The next day, fortunately, any serious activity was out of the question. After the heavy rain two days earlier, the terrain was still awash despite its steepness. Streams ran in every hollow, waterfalls fell in curtains from the cliffs of Mt Hooker, while the peak itself was dusted with fresh snow. The clear air was bitterly cold.

Sitting under the bivvy rock in semi–dark when the sun was out was impossible for long, so I went for a walk in what was now familiar territory. A breeze set the tussock blades nodding gently, keas squawked from the hillside above me, and the Solution Range rose beyond the flat, friendly and hospitable in the midday sun. Cloud built up around Mt Hooker as I strolled across the flat to the airstrip, a short level stretch of grass cleared of rocks, with the stream at one end and high cliffs at the other: there is no opportunity for aborted landings or late take–offs here. Richard Rayward and Bruce Jenkinson had prepared the strip in 1967, after walking in via Brodrick Pass and the Solution Range, as part of an optimistic commercial hunting enterprise. I admired Richard's courage for landing his plane in such a remote and difficult place, with so little room for error. On the far side of the airstrip, where the stream descends from Docherty or Lower Otoko Pass, was the point where I had left the flat two years ago, feeling sore and demoralised. Now I regarded it with different eyes.

Dawn did its best to break as I crossed the stream near the bivvy rock to begin the long ascent of Mt Hooker. Dark clouds covered the sky, moving in from the west, and Mt Hooker itself was invisible. But there was no wind and it was difficult to tell what the day would bring. Besides, after a rest day, with nothing in my pack except a little food and climbing equipment, I was feeling fit and optimistic, so why not see how far I could get?

On the grassy spur up which I started the ground was soft and slippery from the rain; still, it offered a direct and quick route up to the glacier covering the southern slopes of the mountain. On my right a small branch of the glacier spilled over the cliff edge above and curved out from the rock, its snout hanging in space. Soon it was below me, as my spur continued to the crest of a ridge, where easy rock led right and onto the glacier, which lay lazily here across broad slopes.

The top of the rock was a good vantage point. Below me, in the valley between Mt Hooker and Mt McCullaugh, lay Murdock Creek, not looking nearly so threatening from here. Further south light rain was falling in the forested valley of the Clarke River, while in the distance the lower Landsborough and Haast Valleys were completely closed in. Of the Main Divide peaks only the lower slopes were visible. As I sat a light rain began to drizzle on me too, but in the direction I would be taking a broad expanse of glacier was still visible, rolling down out the cloud that hid the upper slopes of Mt Hooker and straddling the ill–defined ridge I was hoping to ascend. To the right of the ridge the glacier disintegrated into a chaos of broken seracs and crevasses, eroded by the summer's wind and rain, while to the left, dissected by gaping crevasses, it fell away steeply to spill over cliffs below. For the time being, anyway, there would be no option but to continue up my glaciated ridge. But would I be able to reach Mt Hooker's summit ridge? It was late March, after all, and there had been heavy rain, so I had to expect wide crevasses ahead. Nor did the cloud misting and unmisting the mountain flanks suggest that I should push the issue too hard. Yet while I sat deliberating, the slope above me whitened as the cloud cover thinned, allowing watery sunlight to bounce off it briefly, then disappear again.

I slowly climbed up the ridge. There was no stress or danger, only crevasses to lunge or jump over and easy ice walls to scramble up, nothing life threatening. The unbroken neve slopes were coming closer now, though still enveloped much of the time by cloud; just a short section of steep glacier ice up to a rise and I would be there. Of course it was too good to be true. At the top of the rise I was confronted by a huge crevasse that severed the entire ridge from the slope above: an insurmountable obstacle. There was nothing for it but to descend the way I had come.

As I retraced my steps, I looked down into the broken ice–fall on my left. Really, it did not look so bad. Glaciers are funny things. Sometimes, late in summer or autumn, broken areas offer possibilities when the route you had hoped to follow is out of the question. Ice walls and pinnacles collapse on one another, the ice becomes so broken that impassable barriers are reduced to a rubble of iceblocks that fills chasms and levels avalanche gullies. What I saw below looked quite plausible, uncertain at a few points, but certainly worth trying.

So off the ridge and into the ice debris I went. It was as if the glacier lacked the strength to hold itself together and was falling apart. Turning uphill again, I could jump from one ice hummock to the next, crampon around the weathered walls of seracs, and bridge my way out of crevasses. I was enjoying myself; it was a real life game of snakes and ladders. Near the head of the ice–fall a line of high seracs glistened blue and white in the fickle sunshine. Was this another dead end? Not at all. The ice gully up which I was walking led to a cleft between two imposing ice towers, from where the rear of the right hand tower revealed itself to be no more than an easy snow slope, sheltered from the weather by the shadow of its vertical neighbour. I could not literally walk up with my hands in my pockets, but almost. And there, stretching unbroken in front of me, was the smooth neve of the glacier, merging not far away with mist and cloud.

Now the only uncertainty was the weather. The rocky summit ridge of Hooker was up there in the cloud somewhere, I knew, and reaching it was just a matter of following up the snow covered glacier to its shoulder. In the cloud, however, finding the correct way down might be a problem; in poor light my upward tracks would be difficult to trace, for the surface was icy and my crampons were making little impression. A combination of rain and whiteout on the descent could be dangerous. Since there was little with which to mark the route, it was necessary to make the most of what I had: at strategic points I peed in the snow, leaving pale yellow markers that might make all the difference in getting me back to camp before dark.

For the rest, it was just a matter of patience. Mt Hooker is a big mountain. I was completely relaxed as I rose through the cloud. On the summit ridge a cold wind blew and the rock was thickly iced. Most of the time it was impossible to see more than a few metres, as the wind drove cloud against the mountain, depositing still more ice on its crest. Soon I was as rimey as the rock. Where the crest levelled off the cloud parted; it was only then that I realised that I had forgotten something: there is a large gap between the piece of ridge I was on and the summit itself. Still, that was no great matter either, for it only required one abseil and was sheltered from the driving westerly wind.

Summits often seem arbitrary endpoints of arbitrary exercises, and this is particularly so when they are lost in mist. Yet I admit that I was glad to reach this one. Enveloping cloud and buffeting wind intensified its remoteness: it was as if I had not only left human habitation far behind, but also the rivers, the forest and the mountains themselves. I was alone in a cold grey void.

On the descent I did not need my yellow markers after all. As I came down from the shoulder of the ridge, the cloud cleared away, giving me a clear view of the neve, down which it was a carefree stroll to the top of the ice–fall. In the ice–fall itself I could follow the trail left by my crampon points, for the individual holes they had made were still as sharp and distinct as when made in the morning. Ice walls, pinnacles, crevasses, blocks: in the angular afternoon light they were a maze of blue, mauve and white, cut and textured by the elements, framed by the tussock and forest green of the Clarke Valley below.

On the rocks at the end of the glacier I paused to watch the shadows deepen in the Clarke gorges and the late afternoon light play on the Haast River flats in the distance. There was no wind. Faintly, from the gorges below, came the sound of rushing water. Somewhere on the far side of Marks Flat keas were engaged in desultory conversation; perhaps, like me, they were enjoying the late sunshine and wondering what tomorrow would bring. Cloud plumes still blew from the summit of Mt Hooker, yet it looked friendly now, in golden light and in my sense of familiarity.

As it turned out, there was still sunshine to be savoured the next day, even though it was largely a local phenomenon. Crossing Marks Flat there was little of Mt Hooker to be seen, but as I climbed the Solution Range sunlight was dancing on the tussock blades that waved in the wind around me, while in the distance dark clouds boiled over the range from the Otoko Valley. There was no sign of Mt Dechen or the mountains beyond it, the subjects of my daydream of a high traverse. This simply confirmed a decision already made: it would be crazy, with the current weather pattern, to attempt to push through to Mt Cook, let alone continue along the crest of the Hooker Range. The only intelligent option would be to head south-east in the hope that the Landsborough River would still be fordable after the rain, and so reach Brodrick Pass and the Huxley Valley on the eastern side of the Main Divide. From the crest of the Solution Range this seemed plausible: as far as I could tell there was not too much water in the Landsborough, Creswicke Flat at the foot of the pass looked sunny and inviting, and the old Fraser Hut there seemed still to be standing.

Off I went, along the crest of the range, then down to the spur that descends to the lower end of Toetoe Flat. At the bushline, a network of deer trails led off through the trees in all directions, just as in the Clarke valley a few days earlier. Once again it was simply a question of choosing those that seemed to follow the best line down to the valley floor.

From close up the Landsborough River looked much wider and deeper than it had from an altitude of 1200 metres; it was discoloured, too, carrying a lot of silt for a Westland river. I followed down the true right bank in the direction of Creswicke Flat, watching for possible fords on the way. There was nothing that looked reassuring. In the end there was only one option, where the river swerved against the far side of the valley shortly before reaching Creswicke Flat. Even here it flowed fast, with all its water concentrated in one channel, but at least the water was less turbulent than elsewhere, and the channel wider, so with any luck it would be shallower as well. Should I fail to get across, I would be in deep trouble, literally.

I waded in nervously, feeling my way in the water with my ice–axe. Soon swiftly flowing steel–grey water filled my field of vision and its roar filled my ears, leaving me with no reference point but the rushing river. As it rose to my waist slow and cautious movement became out of the question; only momentum could keep me upright against the force of the water now, so I started running, facing the opposite bank, while the current pushed me downstream in the direction of the rapids. Fortunately the bottom was level and its stones too small to trip over, enabling me to keep up my slow–motion run, sometimes making little headway, but approaching the far bank diagonally, a compromise between where I wanted to go and the water was determined to take me. So it was not only the cold that had me shivering when I finally hauled myself to safety up the bank.

When my fear had subsided I felt pleased with myself for those few minutes work. Later, when I had experienced what the weather had in store for me, I would be even more pleased, and relieved at my prudence in deciding not to go up the Landsborough in the direction of Mt Cook. Had I taken that option I might still be there.

As I walked leisurely, boots squelching, towards Fraser Hut, a helicopter flew up the valley along the Solution Range, cruising just above the bushline. The makers of those trails I had followed would be in trouble if they showed themselves. I wished them luck. In the long grass of Creswicke Flat there was another sort of trail to follow: that of the light aircraft which used the airstrip during the summer months, ferrying customers in and out for whitewater rafting tours. The hut itself was a mess: a fireplace, a few dilapidated bunks, some loose sheets of iron, a lot of holes. During a storm, however, it would probably keep me dry, and it was a storm I was expecting, despite the evening sun lighting up the grass outside. Upstream, the entire valley had disappeared in an premature night of cloud, taking all the mountains with it.

During the night, surprisingly, the rain held off, yet in the morning nothing was visible but the river, as dense, threatening clouds hung right down to the valley floor. I could smell the rain. If ever it looked like the makings of a heavy day, this was it, and Brodrick Pass was a long way above me.

By the time I had gone a few hundred metres up the stream draining Brodrick Pass I was in the cloud. A track along the bank made travel pleasant, so pleasant, in fact, that I took no notice how far I had come, and by the time I considered my position was well beyond where I should have crossed the stream to climb the ridge on the other side. Oh well, no matter, for according to the map the ridge on my side should be fine too. The rain began as I started up a steep spur leading away from the stream, and throughout the day it became only heavier. The higher I went, the less shelter there was to be found in the forest from the downpour. At the treeline, where my spur joined the main ridge rising from the river, I was hit by the first blasts of northwest wind, which became fiercer as I climbed up the bare ridge beyond, until I was able to veer right and descend to a basin below the pass.

When I stopped to rest among large boulders, sheltered from the worst of the gale, a tiny rock wren emerged from a crevice. It perched on a rock near my head, hooking its toes into the lichen and bracing its few grams of bodyweight against the storm. As it flexed its knees, bobbing up and down, it shook its head at the sight of the large creature having such trouble staying upright in a bit of wind.

Humbled, I staggered over to the stream in the centre of the basin to start the climb beside it for the pass, making sure that I did not stop again until out of the rock wren's sight. Luckily the wind was behind me now and helped me up the final slope, but on the pass itself the blasts were impossible to withstand; I had to crouch low as each gust passed, then scurry forward a few paces before the next one hit, keeping a good grip on the rocks lest the gale blast me head first into the Huxley Valley. Once away from the crest of the pass, however, the wind eased and being blown away began to seem less likely. The slope became grassy, I could stumble and slither down anywhere, while in the gloom below, at the edge of the first patch of bush in the valley, Brodrick Hut beckoned.

All night the storm raged. The wind screamed and torrential rain lashed the hut. But inside was paradise: secure, dry and warm – and with a mattress to sleep on! Moreover, I had been in the Huxley Valley before and knew that there were swingbridges where the river had to be crossed, so now there was nothing that could stop me from getting out to the road–end. And since I had that mountain radio I could get a message through to Frank Dore asking him to come and pick me up. In the knowledge that I was safe, I could even enjoy the storm.

At dawn it stopped. The wind had swung to the south, the sky was clear and still, and valley mist hung in the trees by the hut. As I descended the winding track above the river, I could hear the boulders tumbling down its bed, swept along by the current. In the absence of a bridge at Huxley Forks it would have been a long wait for the river to become fordable; and the thought of what the Landsborough River would be like now made me feel queasy. The lower Huxley too could be crossed by swingbridge, opening the way to the Hopkins River, now a broad sheet of water covering its bed from one bank to the other. Then it was only an hour to the road–end. When Frank drove up from Lake Ohau later in the day, he found trout lying in the middle of the road, left stranded by receding floodwaters.

CHAPTER NINE

Be melting snow.
Wash yourself of yourself.

A white flower grows in the quietness
Let your tongue become that flower
– Rumi

December 1994. There remained the business of traversing along the Hooker Range north of Mt Hooker, which I had 'not–climbed' five years previously.

The bus dropped me off at the bend where the highway leaves the Mahitahi Valley, and within a hundred metres of the road I had entered another world, one in which there existed only shades and textures of green: soft, pliant, still, alive, powerful. The forest canopy shut out noise and movement, washing in deeper green the ferns and lichens, the moss that covered tree–trunks and earth alike. On that moss I stepped without a sound, leaving no trace, as if treading on green light rather than the ground. Not even water broke the silence.

Near the bank of the Mahitahi River shafts of sunlight pierced the canopy. Spots of blue expanded and vibrated gently as their circles of leaves merged and divided again. There was the caressing hiss of running water, then its motion, and below me the river appeared, clear and glittering in the morning light. A faint track led along the high bank, biding its time before descending gradually to water level. I moved upstream hemmed in by the embankment and the river's edge, splashing through shallows when bypassing boulders, to reach open flats dotted with totara trees. The cattle grazing there took no more notice of my passage than they did of the river or the valley cloud forming above us.

From the end of the clearing a wide track led through forest to another riverside clearing, where Morse Hut, simply by being there, provided a reason to rest and eat. Another herd of cattle watched me indolently, a

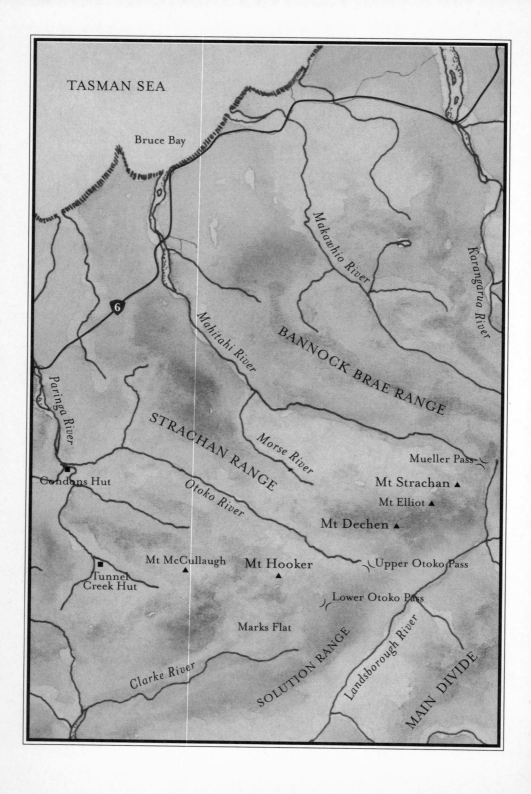

trifle bored. For me, however, the fun was about to begin. Around the next bend the clearing ended abruptly, and with it the sense of being part of a humanised world. Suddenly it became necessary to watch my feet, to think, to observe closely my surroundings and reflect on what they told me. I had to engage with the landscape instead of merely passing through it. Mountain, forest and river compelled me to read their signs and respond to them.

An awkward rocky knoll pressed hard against the river, a reminder, in case I had forgotten, that the bones of the landscape would be shaping my journey just as they gave form to mountain and valley. Then the Morse River joined the Mahitahi, foaming from its side valley over large and slippery boulders; even with a middling flow it was difficult to ford. So water too would be part of the process I was entering, with none too subtle ways of imposing its authority.

Crossing to the true right bank of the Mahitahi – my first real test – presented no problems. The water ran deep but quietly over a smooth bed, one that held no surprises for feet in search of level passage. On the other side, not far above the river, an old deer trail led along the edge of a bush–covered terrace, with now and again a metal marker nailed to a tree–trunk to reassure the traveller that this was in fact the correct path, despite the forest regrowth and windfalls. From a thicket a doe started at my appearance, just as I started at hers, and dashed deeper into the forest. While there was little evidence that she or any of her relatives were putting much effort into track maintenance, most of the time the trail remained visible, requiring only a little deer reasoning to trace in the missing bits as it wound its way along the terrace edge to the small S–bend in the valley.

At the bend the river bed rises to the level of the terrace. Just around the corner, a rock buttress descends from far up the mountainside down to the river's edge; it forced me to cross back to the other bank, where Panel Flat, the last of the Mahitahi flats, lies in the S–bend. River and forest have erased any sign of the airstrip that shooters used here in the days when deer were plentiful. The flat is disappointingly short, too: almost immediately I had to cross back to the true right bank again, in order to follow up that side of the river for the remainder of the day. There was no trail now, only boulders lying in and out of the torrent, and bluffs that forced me into energetic detours away from the river, over awkward rocks and through thick scrub. On the other side an enormous recent landslide tempted me for a while with what, from my laborious route, looked like clear going up the valley. But as any old prospector knows, the going is always better on the far side of the river, just as the biggest nuggets are always at the opposite end of the rainbow. Anyway, the force of the river brawling with its boulders made it easy to resist the temptation; I had made my decision and would accept the consequences.

Daylight was coming to an end as I neared the Edison River junction. No trace remained of the rough shooters' hut that had once existed downstream, nor did there seem to be a good rock shelter on my side of the river, so I camped in an open creek bed. The clear evening sky promised to remain that way, and there was enough grass available between the rocks to sleep comfortably, with my head pillowed by a clump of celmisia and frost forming on the Mt Cook lilies around me.

Rocks overhanging the bank pushed me into the icy river first thing in the morning, just beyond the Edison junction. I was wide awake by the time I reached the opposite bank, where a steep scramble led up to a forested terrace well above the river. One or two old route markers were nailed to trees, but in no time at all the dense cover of ferns and fallen trees had separated me from whatever traces of track there were. Since the hillside above the terrace, relatively free of undergrowth, had a come hither look about it, I headed that way, up through leads in the forest, climbing slowly, past stands of gnarled totara trees, taking my time. Where the trees became sparser, a clear stream bed on my left offered easy passage up past the bushline and into the scrub beyond it, towards a line of bluffs below the snow–covered flank of Mt Strachan. Unfortunately, the helpful stream disappeared under scrub well short of the bluffs, which looked steep and loose anyway, so there was nothing for it but to go where the terrain directed me, climbing still further left, in the direction of a big spring avalanche that ploughed well down into the scrub.

Any plan or precise idea of a route had long since vanished from my mind. (I had started the day with the idea of following the Mahitahi River to its source, climbing to Mueller Pass and proceeding along the range to Mt Strachan from there. That was irrelevant now.) Avalanche debris had flattened enough of the scrub for me to climb over rather than through the tangle, making diagonally for the avalanche gully itself.

Once on the avalanche snow, movement became easier; instead of hauling myself up on branches that refused to stay still just when I needed their support, now I could step with a measured pace, rhythmically, breathing evenly. Although the snow steepened as I neared the bluffs, and the rocks above were vertical, further left again were rock slabs that looked manageable even with the pack I was carrying. So that was the way I went, reaching the top with dignity intact but badly in need of a rest. As I sat on a tussock a kea landed on a rock to bid me welcome and indicate, moreover, that it was quite prepared to share my lunch should I be in need of company. It waited patiently for me to spread out my offerings, selected a piece of salami, then returned to its rock, chewing unhurriedly and methodically, while observing with polite condescension the visitor's droll behaviour. Quickly, however, its interest was exhausted and it flew off, squawking loudly, in search of more intelligent conversation, leaving me to contemplate my surroundings.

I was now 1000 metres above the Edison River junction. Across the upper Mahitahi the peaks of the Bannock Brae Range, still deep in spring snow, jabbed at the sky, sharp overlapping plates of rock set on edge and exposed to the elements. The lower valley was hidden by thick cloud which lay against the mountain walls, while further away at Bruce Bay, where the river runs into the sea, the coastline showed clear and cleanly cut as if with a knife. In front of me rose Mt Strachan. Height–wise, I was halfway between the sea and the mountain's summit, and from where I stood its broad flank, heavily covered in snow, swept upward, disappearing not far above me into the cloud blown over its summit by a southerly wind. What I could see looked easy, not much more than a steep walk diagonally up the mountain, still following the lie of the land, still tending left, and on up into the cloud where, no doubt in due course, all would be revealed. The soft snow, knee–deep, made progress slow. Soon consciousness narrowed until nothing remained other than the next step to be taken and the texture and pattern of the snow, its whiteness passing gradually beneath me, crystalline and heavy with water, its luminosity changing as swirls of cloud extended and retreated overhead. I rested frequently, turning to reflect on the line of footprints rising from far below, in a winding curve, to the purple plastic boots that kept me secure on the mushy surface. Time and sound ceased to exist; there was only snow and sunshine unfolding without end.

As the afternoon warmed, the cloud about me dissolved, giving glimpses of rock and ridge, and higher, ice. Eventually I reached the edge of a small glacier descending steeply from the summit, and on its far side climbed rocks to gain the main crest of the Hooker Range, which here separates the head of the Mahitahi from the Zora tributary of the Landsborough. On the Mahitahi side of the ridge, three hundred metres below the summit of Mt Strachan, were some snow–free ledges covered with loose rock. It was a magnificent, airy place to camp, and obviously I would not be the first to do so: the smell of thar was strong. Late afternoon sunlight warmed the rock, while far below the Mahitahi wound its way to the ocean, with remnants of fair weather cloud clinging to its valley walls. The Tasman Sea was calm, a huge mirror extending to the horizon, bouncing still more light and warmth in my direction. It was easy to imagine thar here, enjoying the view, lounging on their ledges, soaking up the last of the sun's warmth before it slid into the sea. The bivouac site was further proof of their impeccable mountain sense.

Nonetheless, I set about rearranging some of the furniture, ejecting large rocks onto the glacier below and laying several flat slabs end to end to make a sleeping platform, which I covered with rope and spare clothing for a suggestion of comfort. I hoped that my hirsute hosts would not hold it against me. After the day's exertions the evening breeze made me shiver, so I crawled into my sleeping bag, cooked dinner, then fell asleep, snug and secure, and stayed that way until dawn.

That the snugness came at a price became clear in the morning when I moved off again and stepped onto the snow. Despite a cold southerly wind blowing from the Landsborough, there was no frost, which with the heavy cover of snow still lying on the mountains meant that my projected traverse of Mts Strachan, Elliot and Dechen would prove a long and tiring day.

The immensity of the landscape unfolded as I climbed towards the summit of Mt Strachan. At my feet the ice of the Strachan Glacier spilled down into the Zora Valley, whose rock walls led down to the Landsborough River, while beyond the Landsborough, in a row, stood the mountains of the Main Divide. To the north lay the ranges of Westland, one after another, snowbound and uncompromising. The northeast was dominated by Mt Sefton and the cliffs of the Douglas Neve below it, with Eagle Peak also visible and looking grander than I remembered it. Above everything, however, rose the navigator peaks: Mt Tasman and Mt Dampier, and higher still the bulk and power of Mt Cook, intimidating even from a distance of thirty kilometres. Everything was silent, bathed in the light and clarity of morning, a stupendous world that would continue forever to reshape itself through the convection of molten rock, the power of water, the passage of wind and time.

From Mt Strachan's summit the world became vaster still, as to the west land gave way to ocean and ocean merged with sky, in gradations of blue, green, aquamarine. Right before me the bulk of Mt Dechen dominated earth and air, with glaciers sweeping down towards the Landsborough on one side and the Edison River on the other. Between us ran the connecting ridge that was to give me passage over Mt Elliot and unnamed summits. It appeared friendly enough: some steep rock sections, a few unknowns, but nothing I could see that looked too demanding; and with a clear sky above and valleys 2000 metres deep on either side to warn me if I strayed from the crest, losing my way should not be an issue.

I set off. The descent from Mt Strachan was pleasant. Away from the eastern slope of the mountain, on the actual crest of the range, the snow was windblown and firm. Crampons bit securely into the surface, making movement almost effortless; only changing snow consistency and a few crevasses dissecting the ridge required attention. Now there was a small rock peak to negotiate. Over or around it? I chose the latter, traversing on the Landsborough side of the range. The snow was steep and extremely soft, and scary with a heavy load. I had to tread each step down methodically into the snow and allow it to set before putting my weight on it. Time appeared to slow as I negotiated wet powder that seemed bottomless yet adhered somehow to this rock face high above the junction of the Zora and the Landsborough, where seven years earlier I'd had my whitewater swim. It looked inviting down there now. But in reality it took only a few minutes to traverse that dangerous snow, then I could amble up a gentle slope to the rock of Mt Elliot.

Where the rock rose sharply, I took the precaution of leaving behind my pack, fastened to the other end of the rope. As it turned out, the holds were big and plentiful. The only serious obstacle was the metre–long ice feathers deposited by the wind on the rock's western edge, which had to be cleared away in order to gain the top and haul the pack up after me.

he right of the ridge crest, snow slopes disappeared in the direction of the Edison River, while, on the left, cliffs fell away to a glacier whose buckled sheets of broken ice reached down to the forest, below which the Landsborough Valley wound its way into the distance. Even from my vantage point 2000 metres above it, the valley looked unending; no wonder I had been glad to reach Kea Flat that night. The valley was free of cloud and a southerly wind continued to blow from it, cold and persistent, but not so strong as to set me on edge. I could relax, at ease in my surroundings, content in the pleasures of precise movement through a spectacular landscape. From the summit of Mt Elliot snow led down to the next gap, then the ridge continued up and down, over rock pinnacles and snow crests, to descend a kilometre later to a broad snowy col at the foot of the northeast ridge of Mt Dechen. There sun–warmed rocks out of the wind offered a comfortable place to rest, eat and meditate on my position.

There are moments when the configuration of world and self seems perfect, when everything seems so rightly placed that it triggers an overwhelming sense of order and harmony, when the world appears perfect, whole, and we understand our place in it. Depending on our intellectual predispositions, we may interpret these moments as a revelation of higher knowledge, a sense of perfect belonging, or sheer animal contentment. They are more likely to occur when we are alone, free from the distractions of sociability, than in the company of others. When we relate to the universe, it appears, there is little room for anyone else.

Nature mysticism is an appealing mode of understanding; the experience of a complete merging of self and the natural world can be powerful and compelling. To be so completely at home that there no longer remains any distinction between self and surroundings; to feel that the pulse of our blood is inseparable from the shafts of sunlight and rain clouds dispersed by the winds, an expression of the same force that trembles in the roots of totara trees as they split the rocks; to sense individual existence as a momentary vortex in an unending process of change: these things are difficult to convey to those who have never experienced them. So the temptation is to insist that such experiences lie beyond words, perhaps even beyond understanding, to invest them with mystery or supermundane significance.

Yet most of the time, in mountain travel, mystical union is not only difficult to achieve, it is also dangerous to pursue. While it may appear attainable in moments of tranquil contemplation, it is difficult to experience a sense of harmony with sweat running into your eyes, your feet hurting, or your teeth chattering with cold; and mystics who try to travel in the mountains, as opposed to merely contemplating them, tend to be short–lived. An inexplicable sense of belonging that is achieved in a thunderclap of enlightenment may prove fatal if it is regarded as a substitute for the close familiarity gradually acquired through more mundane forms of interaction. Seeing oneself as a momentary vortex in the process of change is all very well, but why make the moment shorter than it needs to be?

When it comes to mystical understanding and union with the cosmos, I prefer the way of action to the way of contemplation, absorption of the self through purposeful action within the world in preference to reposing in meditation outside it. The kinds of action we can pursue are many; while mountain travel works for me, others achieve the same end through such activities as gardening, sailing or the performance of good deeds. What matters is that the activity is practised to the point where it no longer requires deliberation, where it becomes instinctive, so that we reach a state in which knowledge is intuitive and informs the action without the intermediacy of words or predetermined structures, thus rendering it fluid and adaptive. Attention then becomes so focused on the doing that the doer disappears from consciousness, and self and surroundings become one in the immediacy and exhilaration of the action. In such rare states the senses are fully receptive to every cue and signal from the environment, and there is no longer any occasion for self–reflection or self–preoccupation. Judgement becomes instantaneous and unerring, and action so prompt that it precedes full consciousness.

If some allow the world to absorb the self, others project the self onto the world. Mountains are reduced to a frame for the portrait of the glorious ego, a doormat on which feet are wiped in order to enter the hall of fame. Yet when the self is projected onto mountains the danger is acute; we become cocky, blasé, and hubris follows. The self stops listening to what the environment is saying.

On Mt Dechen it is difficult to have illusions of grandeur or to forget who is boss. Although its height of 2643 metres is modest, its bulk is colossal, an enormous protuberance which catches and cools the moisture–laden winds that blow from the ocean, triggering the snowfalls that cap its summit with ice and coat its massive flanks with steeply falling glaciers. Its northeast ridge, though technically easy and relatively short, feels like a big undertaking, and, coming at the end of four kilometres of high ridge from Mt Strachan, is a long way from anywhere except the clouds that form over it.

It was slow going. The ridge was sheltered from the cold airstream by Mt Dechen itself, so at first the snow was wet and heavy, and I sank in up to my knees. Small crevasses needed care, but the higher I went, the harder the surface became, and steeper too. Taking small steps, I climbed so slowly that motion was imperceptible; I seemed to be marking time on the surface of infinity, a tiny figure ascending the curve of an immense sphere of white crystal, like an insect on the surface of one of those spherical snow scenes encased in glass, a terrestrial creature tapping on the outside of the dome of heaven. White beneath, blue above: it went on forever.

A gust of wind brought me back to earth. It plucked off my hat and sent it skimming towards the Landsborough, threatening to send me with it. Moments later the wind had stopped again. On the summit everything was still and clear, and I could see that I had not, in fact, been treading my way among the stars: I was still in South Westland, for to my right was the Tasman Sea, while in front of me, across the head of the Otoko Valley, was Mt Hooker, with its long east ridge descending to Docherty Pass. At my feet a smooth glacial plateau, two kilometres wide, with not a crevasse in sight, sloped gently down towards the upper Otoko. On skis the descent would have taken only a few minutes; but walking down was easy too: I could have descended with my eyes closed, so wide and smooth was the snow that led down to the edge of the plateau and the rocky ridge that links with Otoko Pass and the beginning of the Solution Range.

By the time I was faced with the task of descending the rocky ridge, I discovered that I had had enough. My high camp on the other side of Mt Strachan was now six kilometres behind me, and during my shuffling, rudderless descent from Mt Dechen I had relaxed completely. I did not feel like concentrating again, yet I had to. Spring snow lay over the upper rocks, a treacherous surface that would render me Landsborough–bound should I tread carelessly. When for ten metres or so I was forced to descend on the rope, the effort of unpacking and then restowing it irritated me. In this frame of mind it seemed pointless to traverse the bump on the ridge known as Mt Gorden. The top of a snow–filled gully leading directly down into the Otoko looked inviting, so I went that way, taking big strides in wet snow which avalanched off in front of me. Where the angle of the slope eased, the avalanche slowed to walking pace and I overtook it again, so with the entire gully moving around me I descended to the valley floor, near the edge of the gravel expanse that was once Otoko Lake.

Close by was a comfortable, well used bivvy rock, but since its shadow was cold and uninviting I stretched out in the grass beside it, drinking, eating and relaxing in the sun's warmth. When evening fell I did not move, I simply remained where I was and crawled into my sleeping bag, with a bottle of water on one side and a snack on the other. The sky was alight with stars and meteors slashed the dark: the dome I had trod that day clearly was not the highest heaven; far beyond it there were countless other wonders.

At dawn there was no dew, even though the sky had remained clear. I lay comfortably on the grass, watching the day gather strength, enjoying the silence disturbed only by keas squabbling in the distance. How different this from my previous visit; how reassuring it felt to be in familiar territory, to know what lay ahead on the descent of the valley. Perhaps the keas I could hear were those that had tried to evict me from their rock dwelling on the far side of the stream. I had heard more about their territoriality since then. Tony Condon had encountered them while venison shooting here during the boom years. He and his partner were using a Tiger Moth to fly the deer carcasses out from a steep little landing strip not far down the valley, which upset the local keas. The Tiger Moth, like all its kind, was sheathed in canvas, and while the little aeroplane was parked on the strip the keas with their strong beaks shredded its outer layer. This left the hunters with a long walk down the valley and complicated repairs before they could become airborne again.

The head of the valley was still in shadow when I crossed the old lake bed and set off down the valley. Here too change has been rapid. In the 1930s, the McCardell Glacier on the flank of Mt Dechen calved into a large lake dammed by an old moraine wall, filling its waters with icebergs. Since then the glacier has retreated so far up the valley wall that it would require one of those ancient siege catapults to lob its ice anywhere near the lake

117

bed. However, any such effort would be useless because the lake itself has disappeared. During a fierce storm the moraine wall holding back the water collapsed and the entire lake decamped in a flash flood that scoured the Otoko Valley all the way to the sea.

My trip down the valley was more leisurely: a brief wrestle with alpine scrub near the river, then the neglected deer trail, intermittent, lost then found again, across side streams, over boulders, through windfalls. At Stag Flat the remains of a recent shooters' camp had been added to the debris of earlier visitors. Presumably it was this party that had taken the trouble to mark and recut some of the trail downstream. Unfortunately their enthusiasm for the task appeared not to have lasted long, for at the first big side creek the track disappeared again. Nonetheless, Reynolds Flat turned up soon enough, and from the foot of Reynolds the old bridle trail had been recut too, so I bypassed the site of my bivouac among the river boulders without seeing it. This time the going was easy, even near the end of a long day.

At its last bend before the beginning of the flats, the Otoko River runs hard against a vertical embankment of old river gravel on the true right bank. The river was so high with snow melt that there was no question of crossing to the other side, as I had done last time. What was more, cloud had been building up all afternoon and the sky looked ominous. So I followed the track on the true right bank to an old hut in a clearing.

Passage here is regarded by those with local knowledge as something of a test piece in route finding. 'No trouble getting to/from Reynolds?' they enquire casually, knowing full well that most travellers do have trouble. Not only is it necessary to stay on top of the old terrace against which the river presses, there is also the matter of having to negotiate an annoying stream bed with vertical sides of earth, smaller versions of the embankment the Otoko River itself is eroding. Here an ice–axe and even crampons may come in handy, especially when it is raining and the banks are muddy.

The old Otoko hut was revolting. Everything was covered in possum shit – mattress, floor, fireplace, cooking bench – and all the mosquitoes of the district seemed to gather there, revelling all night long in the heavy humidity and the lightning shaking the ranges. 'Try feeling mystical now, my friend', you may wish to comment. The point is taken, yet neither mosquitoes nor possum shit seriously upset my equanimity.

But it was different in the morning. The rain – cold, hard, heavy – began as I left the hut. At this point I discovered that my high–tech parka had given up the ghost, so that within fifteen minutes I was soaked through and bitterly cold. Rain in the mountains overnight had raised the river level even further. All I could do was to continue along the true right bank, splashing along muddy cattle tracks, through forest bowed down by water, storm clouds almost down to the river and the rain driving in my face. The highway remained invisible until I was right beside the Paringa Bridge. Local DoC workers gave me a lift to the Lake Paringa Cafe, where I was invited to sit by the fire to wait for the northbound bus. When it came three hours later I was still shivering.

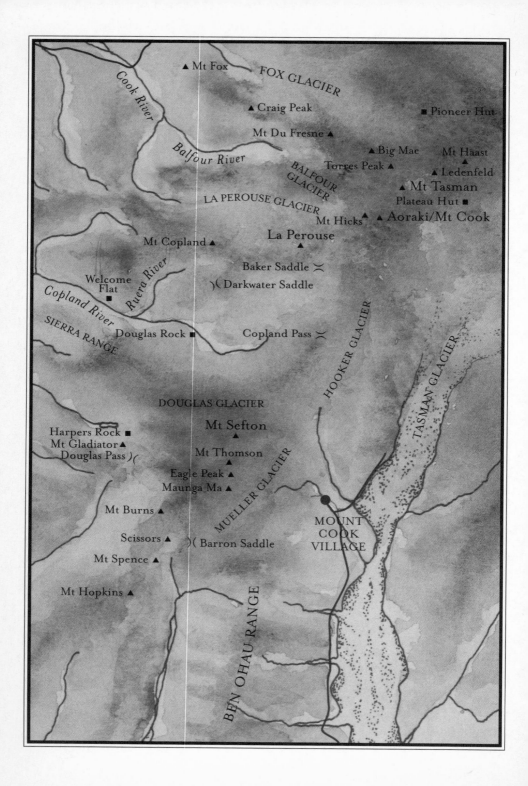

CHAPTER TEN

Poor gentleman, he droops apace,
You plainly find it in his face:
That old vertigo in his head,
Will never leave him, till he's dead:
Besides, his memory decays,
He recollects not what he says;
He cannot call his friends to mind;
Forgets the place where he last dined:
Plies you with stories o'er and o'er,
He told them fifty times before.
How does he fancy we can sit,
To hear his out–of–fashioned wit?
But he takes up with younger folks,
Who for his wine will bear his jokes:
Faith, he must make his stories shorter,
Or change his comrades once a quarter...
– Jonathan Swift, *Verses on the Death of Doctor Swift*

After my journey up the Mahitahi and down the Otoko I got it into my head to try Mt Cook again. I felt fit, and in the centenary year of the first ascent it was twenty–one years since I had been on the High Peak. In the interim both Aoraki and I had changed.

For a start, both of us were thinner on top, though according to this measure I appeared to have withstood the mauling by time rather better than the mountain. While my hair has gradually been disappearing, I can still reassure myself that what remains is silver rather than grey, and that when the wind blows from the right quarter I can still look as wild and woolly as Beethoven.

For Aoraki, on the other hand, the thinning process has been cata-strophic. The massive landslide of 2 December 1991 demolished the top of the High Peak and much of the East Face, sending millions of tonnes of rock and ice down into the Tasman Valley, destroying the Hochstetter Ice–fall and everything else in its path, and stopping only after it had begun to climb up the far side of the valley, six kilometres from its starting point. It left the summit 10.4 metres lower than before. Formerly the High Peak had an impressive profile, symmetrical and powerful; now it is gaunt and hollow, its jawline capped by a few wobbly teeth ready to fall out at any moment. In fact, since 1991 the High Peak has ceased to be a fixed entity. As more rock has continued to collapse, the mountain's highest point has been making its way along the summit ridge in the direction of the Middle Peak. Whereas once it was formed by the junction of the North Ridge and the Zurbriggen Ridge, now it is located some fifty metres to the south, at a relatively solid lump of rock on the Summit Ridge.

Nor are these the only indignities that time has inflicted on Aoraki. Climatic change has shrunk its ice–caps and hollowed out its glaciers, and the ice has slipped down around its flanks, leaving the mountain with those characteristic signs of advancing years: a scrawny neck and droopy chest above flabby belly and fat hips. Thus far I have managed to avoid the acuter forms of this sort of metamorphosis, but I have had to cope with human frailties not normally experienced by large geological formations. Some, like varicose veins and dandruff, are not life–threatening conditions; others, such as deteriorating vision and that broken ankle I have com- plained of, are more troublesome in the hills. A crush fracture of the spine – the result of getting caught up in that avalanche in the Haast Glacier – has had no lasting effect, other than making it difficult to turn my head as far to the right as the left, and which luckily is offset by my nose's preference for pointing slightly to the right, a consequence of hitting myself in the face with my ice–axe while jumping a crevasse. (The resulting com- position, an art critic might say, is a creative tension or dynamic balance of assymetries.)

During the twenty–one years since my previous ascent I had actually made a number of attempts to climb Aoraki, but each time the result has been much the same. I would grind my way up the Haast Ridge to the Grand Plateau, or up the Hooker Valley to Empress Hut, discovering en route that I was not as fit, either physically or mentally, as I had wanted to believe. I would wake in the pre–dawn darkness from an uneasy, troubled sleep, step outside in slushy snow or listen to a rising wind, and secretly be glad that conditions did not favour a bid for the summit. The sheer size and steepness of the mountain, looming darkly overhead, would overawe me, for in my heart I knew I was not up to the undertaking. I would retreat the way I had come, wracked by doubts. Why was I so nervous in what was familiar territory? Was I refusing to face up to the fact that I no longer had it in me? Was I just kidding myself?

After traversing Mts Strachan and Dechen, as I say, I felt fit and confident. Besides, Aoraki was in its centenary year, whereas I was only pushing fifty: I figured I must have the advantage.

I managed to hitch a ride by ski–plane into the head of the Franz Josef Glacier, then make my way via the head of the Fox Glacier and Governor Col to the Grand Plateau on the eastern side of the Divide. Weather and snow conditions en route were good, and from the comfort of Plateau Hut things looked straightforward enough. Zurbriggen Ridge rose on the far side of the Plateau, leading directly to the High Peak. Matthias Zurbriggen was not the first to climb Mt Cook, but to reach the summit alone by this route, only a few months after the first ascent, had been a great achievement. I could do a lot worse than to imitate him. Towards evening Gavin Tweedy arrived via the Haast Ridge with same idea. We decided to keep each other company while still climbing independently.

At two in the morning the Plateau was awash with moonlight. We needed no torch to see the crevasses for they cut darkly into blue snow. The surface was frozen, the air still. It was a magnificent night. Yet even before we started up the snow slope at the foot of our ridge, the moon had disappeared behind Mt Tasman, leaving us to pick our way as best we could across avalanche debris, reflecting that we had better be well off the snow face above before the sun got to work on it.

Faced with the problem of getting onto the face, suddenly we no longer felt so sure of ourselves. Ice bulged steeply, split by high walls. It forced us to climb onto the upper wall of a crevasse where it spilled over a big drop, and on one pick swing airily around a corner above. With this behind us, however, the way ahead was clear. The slope rose steeply above, to lose itself among the stars.

Steadily, slowly, we climbed, one foot, one hand at a time, ice–axes and crampons biting firmly into the frozen slope, now tending right, now tending left in order to relieve straining muscles. Our minds focused only on each successive move, nothing more, trying to ignore discomfort, not thinking about how much further or what lay ahead. Our torches cast only small circles of light on the snow in front of our faces; now and again little flurries of spindrift swirled through the beams. The night was still except for the scratching of metal against ice and the sound of our breathing.

At our backs the sky began to lighten, spreading pale blue then red from the horizon and washing out the stars. Snow and ice soaked up colour, and daylight revealed the immensity of the mountain we were climbing. Wrinkles in the ice, rocks jutting out of the slope above, took a long time to reach and pass, while below the world unfolded, range after range taking shape above an ocean of cloud.

A kilometre is a long way when coated in ice and tipped on end. The surface became icier, harder, forcing us to frontpoint more, ice–axes scratching awkwardly. This made us glad to arrive where the ridge merges with the Linda Shelf. Muscles ached, effort and concentration had dried our throats. But as we drank and looked at our surroundings, we knew that Aoraki's 1991 mishap had not diminished them in the slightest. At our feet the ice of the East Face swept down to the Plateau and over its edge to the Tasman Valley below. Over the top of the Main Divide we could see the mountains of Westland, edged with grey cloud that had come in from the sea. The ocean itself was still dark, almost indistinguishable from the coastal plain. Around us the wind whistled, rising from the glaciers below, cold but not strong: just a subtle menace, a reminder that it could do much more than pluck gently at our jackets.

Yet soon the wind faded and the air was still as we moved up the gully to the foot of the summit rocks. The surface kept us on our toes: hard ice, brittle from melting and reforming day and night, forced us to move slowly and take each step with studied precision. I felt resentful at having to make an effort where the going is usually easy. Little setbacks like that are unsettling; they make you feel vulnerable if you're not expecting them. The mountain closes in behind you and presses a cold finger between your shoulder blades: remember!

Nonetheless, the summit rocks themselves seemed to lie back at a gentle angle, warm in the sun, coaxing us upward. When they merged into the summit ice–cap, we were higher than everything around us: now there was nothing standing between us and whatever the weather might choose to hurl in our direction. Fortunately, the air remained still and we were grateful. The ice–cap lifted us still higher, now over snow, now over ice, sastrugi shattering under our feet, its fragments tinkling as they rolled away, until nothing surrounded us but light and air, while in the west, below us, clouds drifted against the foothills and breakers rolled towards the shore.

As a result of the 1991 landslide, Aoraki became 10.4 metres shorter, 3,754 metres, whereas I am still much the same height I was: the unprepossessing 1.69 metres recorded in my passport. Therefore at this stage any impression of shrinkage on my part is subjective, or at most relative, the result of having daughters grow up past me. So I can tell myself I am doing better than Aoraki, that at any rate in human terms I have not suffered comparable damage. But there is one difference of course: whereas I have stopped growing, Aoraki has not. For millions of years to come its rocks will continue to be pushed skyward along the fault–lines that gave it birth, by which time I will be well and truly past my prime. Geologists estimate the maximum rate of uplift in the central Southern Alps at around twenty millimetres per year, which means that in the 1991 landslide Aoraki lost the equivalent of a mere 500 years growth. In other words, leaving aside the possibility of catastrophic earthquakes, asteroid collisions and even the frailty of its rocks, around the year 2500 Aoraki will have regained its former height and robustness, while my remains, along with my name, will have vanished without a trace.

Ou–yang Hsiu, a great writer and prime minister of China during the eleventh century, somehow found time to climb mountains as well as run the empire. While climbing Mt Hua, China's spectacular holy peak of the West, he collected from graffiti on temple walls the names and particulars of those who had climbed it in the 300 years before him. The experience led him to reflect on the impermanence of human affairs:

'... of those five hundred men who came and went, whether earlier or later, some failed in life and some succeeded, some died young and some lived long, and those respects were unlike each other, yet all passed away when their time was up. Their names and the dates of their visit are ravaged by wind and frost, so that while some remain others have already disappeared. All that survives, in the end, is the two thousand metres of mountain rock alone.'

Mt Hua and Aoraki both are located near active geological faults, and have their insides badly shaken from time to time, but whereas Mt Hua is made of solid granite, Aoraki consists of mudstone held together by ice. So I cannot be quite as confident as Ou–yang Hsiu. Yet this much is certain: long after my centre of gravity has been lowered and I have been reduced to rubble, Aoraki (give or take a few dozen metres) will still be standing. While its outline may be dented here and there, it will comfortably fill the horizon, and just as now will cast its shadow out to sea. Its massive bulk will continue to deflect damp seawinds to rain on rimu and kahikatea in the west, and in the east blow away any remaining traces of the late twentieth century. It will survive countless centenaries without being troubled by them in the slightest.

Despite such intimations of mortality, I was nonetheless confident that I had climbed Aoraki better than ever before. I had been more in control, calmer, more alert, more responsive to my environment, more ... what? Self–possessed? That comes close to it. And certainly more focused.

Part of the explanation was the mental and physical preparation involved in having traversed Mts Strachan and Dechen, and some peaks at the head of the Franz Josef Glacier, beforehand, instead of trying to rush onto the big mountains cold, as I have sometimes been inclined to do. Yet that could not be the complete answer. When twenty or twenty–five years old I tended to be in the mountains for three or fours months at a stretch, doing ascents of Mt Cook as part of a long sequence of climbs, yet I had never climbed it as well as I had now. Nor was it just a matter of waking up and feeling right on the day. What was clear was that those long solitary excursions in South Westland were having their effect: movement was becoming instinctive, route–finding and movement over difficult ground rarely required effort, and my dominant mental state had become ease rather than anxiety. It was the result of half a lifetime of effort. That is not to say, of course, that others may not get as far or further in ten or even five years, but simply that in my case it took thirty, and I was content to have got that far.

One complication with progressing so slowly is that by the time you get your head together, your body starts to pack up, or at least begins to demand more considerate treatment than it has received hitherto. However, that is just part of a much greater difficulty. The fact is that there is no neat linear progression, no steady accumulation of wisdom or skill; the whole business is so beset with uncertainties and ambiguities that there are occasions when every day seems like a new beginning. When the mountains change so rapidly (weather, climbing conditions, erosion, climate change) and we change along with them (mood, mental baggage, fitness, ageing) it becomes difficult to feel certain about anything. What is more, the scope for doubt and uncertainty becomes larger still when we go into the mountains alone, when there is no one else present with whom we can compare performance or discuss the conditions encountered. Then having a bad day can result in serious self–doubt.

In February 1999 I came to the mountains with a typical scheme in mind, hatched, as so often is the case, in a vacuum, without the mountains present to constrain the fantasy: I would go up the Hooker Glacier, climb La Perouse and go down its west ridge to the head of the Cook River, then climb Mt Copland and descend on its southern side to Darkwater Saddle and eventually the Copland Valley. February 1999 was a hot month, at the end of a long summer in the wake of a series of snow–lean winters. Global warming was evident everywhere.

I started up the East Hooker Track with the sun hot overhead and shade nowhere to be found; under a heavy load, progress was slow, involving much sweating and blowing. The terminal lake of the glacier looked huge, larger than I had ever seen it. Across the glacier I could see, too, why what was once the main track is now so little used. Erosion had turned what had once been little gullies descending across the track into dangerous, virtually uncrossable canyons, leaving Hooker Hut perched on an isolated vestige of glacier terrace, separated from the glacier itself by a high moraine wall that looked even more steep and dangerous to climb than moraine walls usually are. Once more the hut has been moved back from the edge to prevent it falling down to the glacier, but this time it has been shifted right back to the very foot of the ridge and it will not be moved again.

A night out under the stars, beside the stream below Mt Mabel, was pleasant; the effort involved in continuing up the glacier the following morning much less so. Reality was starting to impinge upon my fantasy. I was moving very slowly, and after the previous day's modest exertions was inordinately thirsty: not good signs.

Despite the snow–free winters and the lateness of the season, climbing through the ice–fall was surprisingly easy, so I could not use that as an excuse to give up. However, the problem of finding a way off the glacier and onto the rock leading up to Gardiner Hut was real and time–consuming: the gap between the ice edge and the foot of the rock gaped wide and uncrossable. The only option that remained was also unattractive; somehow I had to climb a little higher up the main stream of the glacier, to where it spilled past the rock wall, and hope that a way onto the rock would be available there. This meant I had to climb a vertical wall of ice; not particularly high, true, but with large holes in the ice below it disappearing into the groaning bowels of the glacier, it was scary enough. That brought me onto a flat little island of ice which, as I had hoped, on its far side hung over the lowest point of the rock, near where it disappeared beneath a shambles of broken seracs. I abseiled off an ice–screw fixed into the surface, remembering only when dangling in space well out from the overhanging ice that I still had a heavy pack on my back. This now did its best to tip me upside–down and eject me from the rope sling in which I was sitting. Desperately I fought to keep myself horizontal until I could touch down on the rock below, to slump there in an undignified quivering heap. After this, hauling myself up to the hut was a pathetically slow affair and I kept a tight grip on the steel cables fixed in the rock for support.

By the time I reached the hut it had become all too clear that a change in plans was required. Physically and mentally, my performance so far had been (I did not want to be too hard on myself) less than optimal; it was an enormous effort to walk to the toilet behind the hut, never mind traversing La Perouse and Mt Copland. Fortunately the view from the hut showed that my original scheme would be impossible anyway. The main stream of the Hooker Glacier was bare of snow and badly broken until well past the base of La Perouse, while further up the valley, towards Empress Hut, the glacier was dissected by huge crevasses running from one side of the valley to the other. Even getting to the head of the Hooker Valley, therefore, would be a struggle. La Perouse itself was almost devoid of snow, its glaciers clinging desperately to the surrounding rock walls – shrivelled, bare, broken and uninviting. It would require a lot of luck and more determination than I could muster to find a way through the breaks, and I knew from past experience that without a decent coating of snow and ice to hold them together the rocks of the Main Divide leading out to La Perouse are extremely dangerous.

So it was time to scrap Plan A and turn to Plan B. I would scale down my ambitions, cross Baker Saddle into the Strauchon Valley, climb Mt Copland from Darkwater Saddle, then travel through new territory by descending the Ruera River to the Copland Valley.

As it turned out, to reach the foot of Baker Saddle was a major undertaking. Never had I see the Hooker Glacier so broken. I was forced to climb in and out of crevasses and balance on sharp ridges of smooth unyielding ice. It was touch and go. The slope up to Baker Saddle was unrecognisable. It used to be snow from top to bottom; on my last visit it had taken me no more than two minutes to descend by starting a wet snow avalanche at the top and glissading down in its track. Now half the slope was shattered rock, the rest of it hard ice severed by huge bergschrunds. As I climbed my confidence fell even lower. What was the matter with me? Was it really just the conditions, or had I crossed, unawares, some threshold in the ageing process compelling me to turn to harmless suburban pursuits such as gardening and stamp collecting?

The descent on the Strauchon side of the saddle was even worse. Once upon a time getting down the Strauchon Glacier was easy even late in the summer. Avalanches off Dilemma Peak on one side and La Perouse on the other would meet in the middle of the glacier, sweeping much of its upper reaches and filling in any crevasses that appeared. Although the avalanches were not frequent, for a safe passage down the glacier, timing was all. Now the glacier was a moth–eaten affair pierced by holes revealing the bedrock below, weeping sores that would take more than one winter's snow to bandage and heal. The further I descended the more broken the ice became, forcing me to climb under rotting arches and teetering seracs, then abandon the ice altogether by abseiling onto the foot of the rock face of La Perouse and scrabbling down there for a hundred metres, before clambering back onto the ice lower down. The descent to the moraine, which on other occasions had taken at most half an hour, now took four hours and consumed whatever nervous energy I had left.

The trek down the moraine–covered lower reaches of the glacier was interminable. As I lay on a flat rock somewhere near the middle of what appeared an endless sea of broken stone, resting, a kea landed beside me and stood observing for a while, no doubt having deduced from my limp form that I was about to kark it. When this took too long it flew off again, shrilly voicing disappointment at my performance. The ascent of the moraine wall and steep snowgrass to the terrace below Darkwater Saddle took a long time too, so that by the time I had located a reasonable bivvy rock the afternoon was well advanced.

Where had the day gone? What was the matter with me? Of course I kept telling myself that conditions were terrible, even unprecedented, but I had believed that I was as familiar as anyone with the Strauchon Valley, and knew that it was reasonable travelling. Was it then a case of my own unfitness bouncing flabbily up against those unprecedented conditions, or was my memory playing tricks on me and the Strauchon Valley had never been as I thought I remembered it?

Knowledge from experience is not obtained under laboratory conditions; it is never a case of repeating an experiment, controlling all the variables until we get consistent results. Each journey, even through the same terrain, is a new exercise, a different undertaking. How often do we say to ourselves, 'I have been here before yet everything seems different; I simply don't recognise the territory'? A journey in rain is quite unlike traversing the same place in sunshine; a ridge ascended when hungry and tired is longer and steeper than the same ridge climbed fresh.

We think we are aware – we *are* aware, to some degree – that our knowledge is always limited, derived from a finite set of experiences. We appreciate that there is always the possibility that next time we will encounter the unexpected, conditions or circumstances unlike anything we have had to cope with before. The gradual extension of the range of what we know and can anticipate is precisely what we call learning from experience. It is based on the realisation that in the flow of reality we are perpetually faced with what is new, and that we must not allow ourselves lazily to lapse into thinking in terms of stereotypes and approximations. We have to pay close attention to what is new and unexpected in each situation as well as what is familiar and routine. Deriving knowledge from experience is not a matter of generating universal principles from it, but rather developing a sensitivity to its modulations, an understanding of what is possible as well as what is likely.

It is one thing to pontificate about these things while sitting comfortably at home, it is quite another to do so while lying prostrate under a rock below Darkwater Saddle, with barely energy enough to light the stove and the setting sun reflected by Aoraki warning that tomorrow will be another hot day. Then it is easier to feel resentful and hard done by: 'How dare the glacier be so broken? It really is unreasonable'; and to wallow in self–pity and doubt: 'I can't handle it any more. Thank goodness my memory is disintegrating along with my body, so at least I can find comfort in delu-sion. It must be time to stop.'

In the morning, however, there was no choice but to go on. The ascent to Darkwater Saddle was strenuous. How was it possible for vegetation to grow on a slope as steep as this? By the time I reached the crest, Plan B had also been burnt away by the sun. The rocks shimmered in the heat; above me on the right, the ridge to Mt Copland rose in smooth slabs and bare glacier ice that glistened nastily in the morning light. It did not tempt me. Anyway, I had already used up most of my supply of ice–screws get-ting down the Strauchon Glacier, so there was a perfectly respectable rea-son for not attempting it.

So Plan C came into action. Meekly I descended on the other side of Darkwater Saddle, then followed the Ruera River down to its junction with the stream draining the Lyttle Glacier. There was Banister Rock, big and comfortable, surrounded by scrub so thick that even from the river bank twenty metres away it is barely visible. Plan C entailed lying under it in the shade and reading my book. I could cope with that. Soon I'd lost myself in the Dublin of Roddy Doyle's *Barrytown Trilogy*. One of the phrases his characters are fond of using seemed to fit my situation particularly well: *fuckin' eejit*.

But hey, I thought, according to the map it is only two kilometres further down the Ruera to Welcome Flat, so by lunchtime tomorrow I should be sitting in the hot pools at Welcome Flat Hut. That is a great way of cheering oneself up.

How was I to know that the Ruera had one final humiliation in store for me. Almost as soon as I left the bivvy rock, large boulders forced me away from the river and into scrub thick and tangled, and not to be rushed. Hakeke, tupare, ribbonwood, groundsel, fuschia, ferns: they competed for ground space, but were all in league to block my progress. While I told myself that the going would get easier once the alpine scrub gave way to forest, it only got worse. The valley sides above the river became steeper and the vegetation burlier. Under the cover of tall scrub, ferns grew so thickly that I could not see where I was putting my feet; often I felt rather than saw the vertical drops below me. Repeatedly I struck scrub so dense that it was impossible to push through; then I would follow a lead down to the river, where I might progress for forty or fifty metres until a deep pool or an overhanging bank forced me into the bush again, clawing my way up roots and branches until it was possible to traverse further across the hillside. Another band of impenetrable scrub would push me to the edge of a moss–covered bluff, and I would have to backtrack to find a route below it, then climb once more until the tangled undergrowth drove me back to the river. In 1931 Alec Graham spent three days cutting a track to get the party he was guiding up the Ruera Gorge. Now there was no trace even of a deer trail, let alone a human one.

It demanded infinite patience. My pack continually got hooked up on branches and I expended a lot of energy freeing it. I spent a lot of time sitting, resting, recovering from my tussles with the scrub. Sweat ran off me liberally; I drank from nearly every stream I crossed, and from the river as well, despite its heavy suspension of glacial silt. Because my glasses kept being steamed up with sweat and knocked off my nose, I packed them away, which made it harder to see where I was going and further diminished my sense of control.

Somewhere along the way, the scrub was displaced by trees and other forest species, but this made little difference to my progress; it remained a slow–motion struggle all the way. I tried the river again. For thirty metres the bank was negotiable, then a huge overhanging boulder blocked further descent to what looked like another fifty metres of clear going. That seemed worth an abseil. As I balanced on the rock at the upper edge of the over-hang, my feet slipped on moss and I crashed heavily against the face of the rock, tearing the muscles in my right arm. The hoped–for fifty metres turned out to be only half that distance, before impassable boulders turned me up the hillside again.

And so it continued for twelve hours. It was late in the day when I reached the final side creek and followed it down to the river. From there I could see the grassy beginning of Welcome Flat – so close that in my desire to be out of the gorge I felt I could almost touch it – perhaps only ten minutes away, were it easy going. But now further progress down the true left bank of the river was barred by a nasty bluff; not high, yet I could not see any way of climbing it without using up much more energy than I had left to call upon.

Here the opposite bank promised easier going; a few boulders, certainly, but back from the river the valley wall had already relented, apparently permitting flat travel to that beautiful grassy clearing which could not be more than 500 metres away. My attempts to cross the river came to nought. With much heaving and grunting I manoeuvred a big log into position to bridge a gap between two rocks over the thundering water, only to have it washed away in seconds. There was just one sensible option: to camp where I was, on a small patch of gravel among the boulders. I was too tired to go any further and felt incapable of thinking the situation through. The likelihood of doing something silly was great, therefore it was best to wait until morning.

At first light the river level was much lower, for the cool night air had slowed the glacial melt of its source. Now it was easy to bridge the stream with a tree–trunk, and in less than an hour after packing up camp I was stumbling across the grassy clearing where the Ruera flows into the Copland River, feeling dazed and humbled. There is nothing like a close encounter with a Westland gorge to put life into perspective. As I followed slowly down beside the Copland towards Welcome Flat Hut, I had time to ruminate on my performance.

Oh, I know, when conditions are tough, getting out in one piece is not a bad achievement. All the same, I could not suppress doubt. Was is it really the conditions, or did it have more to do with being fiftyish and fattish? Did I really go into the hills alone because I enjoy solitude or was it because I could not bear anyone to witness my decline? Did I prefer to climb alone for the intellectual and emotional experience it yielded or because I knew that fit companions would leave me floundering in their wake, or laugh at me because I had forgotten how to tie the knots that any competent climber ties? Oh woe is me.

That is one of the problems of travelling in the mountains alone: doubts and uncertainties are more likely to trouble the solitary individual than the social animal. It is more difficult, when alone, to correctly judge the extent to which the changes we perceive are in ourselves or our surroundings, the extent to which the problem that needs to be faced is glacial retreat, forest growth, weather conditions, or a mild hysteria brought on by evidence of bodily decrepitude. Sometimes it is invaluable to be able to discuss conditions as you encounter them, to compare notes, to scrutinise the faces of your companions for evidence of the pain and hardship you yourself are experiencing.

What I needed, as I lurched along the bank of the Copland River and splashed through the shallows, was a companion to say: 'For God's sake man, stop your whining. You're not getting any younger, but neither are you dead yet. Conditions are bloody awful, the weather is hot, and I've been struggling too. You'll do better next time, especially if you make more effort to get into shape beforehand.'

CHAPTER ELEVEN

...the impulse which impells some people to search for knowledge in the wild is for the benefit of the world, and cheaply bought at any price. Fools say that knowledge can only be acquired from books & men cribbing, as it were, [what] other people thought – and call me a fool & even worse for wasting my time in mountain solitudes.... I have now been wandering about the uninhabited parts of New Zealand for over five & thirty years always finding something in nature new to me and the world.
– Charlie Douglas, *Waiatoto–Copland Notebook*

Evening. The setting sun lit up the snow on Scott Peak and Mt Sefton; lower down the cliffs of the Sierra Range were already lost in shadow. Cool air was gathering above the river and drifting into the forest to coalesce with the growing dark between the trees. It touched bare skin in shivers, hinting that autumn was not far away.

Welcome Flat Hut was deserted and still. After a siesta I was feeling better, at any rate able to cope with a hot bath, so on bare feet I padded along the track to the hot pools. There was no one else about, only the hot spring bubbling at the bush edge and in the open the pools themselves, steaming gently and diffusing the smell of sulphur. I stripped and waded into the deepest pool, sludge oozing between my toes and rising to the surface as mineral soup. Near the edge, where a flat stone had been placed on the bottom, I sat down, leaning against the bank. The heat penetrated tired muscles, dissolving my aches as quickly as the sludge in the pool settled, and dispersing just as rapidly any murmur of remaining energy. I sat lethargically, watching bubbles rise to the surface, stirring only to dislodge persistent sandflies from my face.

The distant sound of the river accentuated the quiet of the evening. In the cool air the steam formed a light mist that wafted over the surface of the pool. It merged with the fog in my brain, and when I turned I saw Charlie Douglas sitting beside me in the water (at least I think it was beside me: in the fog it was hard to tell). His weathered face creased in a friendly smile; his long grey hair hung wetly and his beard floated in the water like kelp.

AV: Am I glad to see you, Charlie. I could use some sympathetic understanding.

CD [*still smiling*]: I beg your pardon. According to my understanding of the classics, the souls of the dead receive sacrifices of wine and meat to enable them to speak. But perhaps in the present situation we may overlook the formalities. However, I should advise that your summons departs from established procedure. Aristophanes called a poet back from the dead to save Athens from her folly; I have never heard of anyone calling on a long departed explorer for assistance.

AV: I'm feeling sorry for myself in South Westland, not fighting a crazy war against Sparta. Anyway, I'm sure Aristophanes would approve the setting: these towering cliffs and black shadows, this water and steam bubbling up from the yellow springs and subterranean realms. It could easily be a scene from *The Frogs*. [*He recites:*]

Brekeke–kex, ko–ax, ko–ax,
Ko–ax, ko–ax, ko–ax!
Oh we are the musical frogs!
We live in the marshes and bogs!
Sweet, sweet is the hymn
That we sing as we swim...

CD [*Joins in, stirring up the gas bubbles that break on the pond's surface*]:

Ko–ax, ko–ax, ko–ax!
What, silence our chorus? Ah no!
Let us sing as we sang long ago,
When we splashed in the sun
(Oh, wasn't it fun)
'Mid the weeds and the sedge
At the pond's muddy edge.
If it came on to rain
We'd dive under again

(To avoid getting soaked)
And still harder we croaked,
Till from under the slime
Our subaquaeous rhyme
Bubbled out loud and clear
For all men to hear,
And burst with a plop at the top,
Brepeplep!
And burst with a plop at the top.

AV and CD [*together, childishly*]: Giggle, giggle.

CD: So you have had a hard journey, eh?

AV[*in confessional tones*]: Coming down the Ruera Gorge yesterday took me twelve hours and still I couldn't reach the flats before dark. I don't recall you mentioning any difficulties in your account of 1892.

CD [*pondering*]: Well now, as best I can remember, back then the Ruera was pretty well free of scrub. Most of the gorge was swept by avalanches. Harry Cuttance and I found gravel lying atop the rocks all the way up the river, a sure indication of melted avalanche debris. So I reckon you have to take into account that in those days snowfalls were heavier, and the glaciers further advanced. It appears the bush has had tropical growing conditions of late and has come on some.

AV: I like that explanation. The only other one even halfway convincing is much less flattering. Yes, I'll stick with the climate change hypothesis. Anyway, it fits with the conditions I encountered in the Hooker Valley and the Strauchon. In 1892 the Government sent you up here to find a snow–free tourist route across the Main Divide. Well, stick around a few more years, Charlie; at the rate the ice is melting Baker Saddle may provide you with a mule track yet. The glaciers are retreating so fast you have to run to keep up with them.

 CD: The ice has been shrinking faster than the British Empire. I find it difficult to recognise some of the territory. All the same, I would not discard the ageing hypothesis entirely. How old are you anyway, if you do not mind me asking? You don't look knocked up.

AV: Fifty–four.

CD [*laughing*]: Only a boy. There should be a few years left in you yet.

I managed to keep going longer than that, despite passing more of my up–country time wet and rheumatic; and much of my time in town, for that matter, in a wet and inebrious state.

AV: Perhaps you're right, but sometimes I feel it would only take a stiff breeze to knock me over.

CD [*philosophically*]: The mountains fall down in time, so it should not surprise us when we are levelled in our turn. Sub–lunary mutability not-withstanding, however, I know of no place finer than this. [*He gestures in the direction of the Sierra Range.*] To be able to see it again is a privilege, as is this hot water. Dead and departed I may be, yet my rheumatism still bothers me.

AV: This valley certainly has changed a lot since you explored it in the 1890s. Your old bivvy rock up the valley, Douglas Rock, disappeared in a huge landslide in 1968. Then in 1987 the hot spring here was almost wiped off the map by a big slide. It flattened the brand new hut, but luckily no one was killed. The place looked like a bomb site.

CD: It does put me in mind of the main street of Ross at the height of the gold rush, only here the mud has been allowed to set. Mind, it is reassuring how rapidly the bush grows back. At old diggings and town-ships like Ross and Okarito little remains of those thousands of diggers intent on instant wealth. The bush has reclaimed everything: shafts, huts, empty bottles, flumes, graves. Nature is very forgiving.

AV: She has a lot to forgive. But you're right. It is a mistake to be preoccupied with what seems to us the negative side of change. Landslides, glacial melt, scoured river valleys: it's all happened countless times before and will continue to happen. Better to rejoice than be indignant over the fact that tupare and hakeke are growing thickly over the rocks in the Ruera valley where once there was just avalanche debris and gravel. The genera-tion of life is wonderful, I guess, even when it does knock you about.

CD: I know you would like to be reassured that sometimes we had it easy in the old days. Well, in some respects we did. Once a man could roam about carrying very little: a billy, a box of matches, a dog for flushing out birds. And it was only at river crossings that we were ever required to carry the dog. The pity is that those days of plenty ended so soon. What with wild dogs, cats and weasels destroying the ground birds, the super-annuated explorer was required to carry ever bigger loads. When I reflect

138

upon it now, it surely was a clear signal to stop.

All the same, I believe I would have coped rather well in the period from the 1920s to the 1960s. I am partial to venison, you see, and know which end of a rifle is which. That the bird life was prolific does not mean that it was invariably tasty. Kiwi tastes like the wrong end of a pig cooked in a second hand coffin, and while a kakapo or weka can keep the wolf from the door, there was many a day when a good venison stew would have gone down better than a mouthful of feathers and gristle. Yet it was pleasant to be here in the age of the birds. I am glad to see that the wekas still plague visitors here and instruct them on the vanity of earthly possessions. It will be a sad day when those bush philosophers disappear.

AV: I recall that you did your bit to help the extinction process along. There was some business regarding a soon–to–be–extinct giant mountain kiwi or roa?

CD [*laughing*]: I am unrepentant. Let my critics try crawling through a Westland swamp for days with a sprained ankle and an empty belly, and then have the luck to encounter a pair of well–fleshed roa guarding an egg large enough to be the makings of a man–size omelette. What would they do? Take a photograph and interview them for the *West Coast Times* or the *Hokitika Guardian*? No, they would do what I did: eat the lot. There's a fundamental truth for you: people care little for the environment while they are hungry.

AV: Well, right now the only way I care to interact with the environment is to do what we are doing: just sit here and watch the mountains rise and fall, while the Alpine Fault does its work.

CD: It's a sensible option. Nor should we forget that this water is heated by the movement of the Fault itself. So merely by sitting here and looking at the scenery we are in touch with the process of change.

AV: But Charlie, for all the business about being in harmony with change and the natural order, I know that you struggled at times to cope with physical decline and the need to find meaning when faced with the inevitability of death. Some of what you wrote in 1902, when being rained on in the Waiatoto valley, reads like the mutterings of a man close to despair, who feels isolated and unappreciated, and is desperately trying to convince himself that he hasn't thrown his life away.

CD [*a little embarrassed*]: I should have thrown that notebook away.

We all of us feel sorry for ourselves at times, but self–pity does not make edifying or uplifting reading for others. All that nonsense about being friendless and my work thwarted .... When, the next day, the sun was shining I knew it was untrue. I had good friends: Gerhard Mueller, George Roberts, the Macfarlanes – people who knew how to carry on a conversation even when the rain continued for a week. Politics, history, books, Westland society high and low; there was no shortage of topics. They accepted me as I was, even when the drink got in the way.

They understood what drove me: not the hope of striking it rich, nor renown, nor even the social utility of what I was doing, rather it was the thing in itself, the self–imposed task, a variety of self–expression. My elder brother was a painter of some standing, as you may be aware. Once in a letter I tried to explain that, like him, I too was an artist, and that he, like me, was also an explorer, that we both had visual imagination. In the final reckoning, is it not all imagination? Painting, poetry, mapping, prospecting: are they not different words for the same activity, the business of reaching into ourselves by reaching beyond ourselves, and sharing what we find with others?

I regret only the time I wasted, not the hardships I endured. My failures I cannot blame on others, as I tried to do when steeped in self–pity. I should have written more, aiming higher in what I wrote, and I should have tried harder with my painting. The rigours of my physical life needed more intellectual content to give it sustenance and balance.

Perhaps my difficulty was that in some respects I had it easy. I was a remittance man, even though the remittances were not so frequent as they may have been; I was what you might call an intermittent remittance man. To a degree that freed me from the necessity of earning a living. There was a time at Paringa when I tried my hand at farming. The trouble was I disliked sheep and my relations with cattle were fleetingly cordial at best. So it was just as well that my family kept me supplied with life's necessities, including books.

AV: I get the impression that the conventional picture of you as an increasingly solitary individual finally overwhelmed by loneliness and ill health is a mistake.

CD: If you ask me, was I ever lonely, the answer is of course I was. But the fact is that I became less solitary over time rather than more so.

You see, I came to realise, albeit late in the piece, that I was actually rather fond of society, for all my declamations to the contrary, and that I was not without social graces. It was just that social engagement required a good deal of effort on my part, which meant that I needed periodic relief. I suspect that part of the difficulty lay in the fact that I had never been properly taught to dissemble, to maintain that polite veneer so essential for the functioning of society, and that this was the reason I found it easier to converse with trees than with my fellows.

Perhaps ageing helps in these matters. Whether it is out of necessity or because we are more able to admit that the fault lies in us rather than those about us, as we grow older we become more reconciled with society. The realisation that my exploration days were coming to an end coincided with the discovery that in Hokitika I had many friends. There was no shortage of company: the widow of my former partner from the Paringa days, Mrs Ward, and friends such as Roberts, Arthur Woodham and Dr Teichelmann. By the way, are you aware that Dr Teichelmann was the first to use your route into the Strauchon Valley, over Baker Saddle, along with Reverend Newton, Jack Clarke and Mr Batson of Waiho? He was a capable mountaineer, but regarded that as the least of his accomplishments. Above all he was a humane and intelligent man.

It was well that I had such friends, for towards the end I had need of them. As I recall, in that Waiatoto Notebook you mentioned, when faced with the hard reality of physical decline I tried to cheer myself up by saying that at least I was in good condition mentally, that I was unlikely to die in the manner of Jonathan Swift, from the head down. Ah the irony of fate. Four years later I had my first stroke by the Paringa River, then three years later a second; during the last fourteen years of my life I was to learn all about dying from the head down. So you see, I regard myself as something of an expert on mutability and the need to acquiesce in all that nature hands to us.

[*Silence. Night is deepening; the mountains are lost in darkness. The pool's surface reflects the dying traces of the vanquished sun. Only the sound of the spring and bubbles bursting give a hint of movement.*]

AV: Charlie, while you say you didn't care about the utility of what you did, it seems that you cared a lot. You dismissed mountaineering as self–indulgent and pointless. I recall a letter you wrote to Harper saying that an enthusiasm for mountaineering is a vice that serves no purpose. Are you telling me that there are degrees of uselessness, that some useless activities are more useless than others?'

CD [*good naturedly*]: I actually told Harper that? A man cannot deny the testimony of the written word. What I had in mind was that any activity pursued far enough, regardless of the cost, becomes a vice. And you must remember that what costs one man little costs another his respect or his life. Like drinking, for example. It was mountaineers – with their social vices of rivalry and braggadocio, their compulsion to write books in celebration of deeds that ordinary folks look upon as routine, or at most a topic to bend the publican's ear after a week or two among the ranges – rather than mountaineering as an activity to which I was objecting. Harper was not a total stranger to such extravagance himself. Nor is it difficult to think of more extreme examples, such as that fellow Fitzgerald for instance, with his insufferable conceit and arrogance. The man was quite certain that it was to him, not Tasman or Cook, that the honour of discovering New Zealand belonged; and as to giving credit to the prospectors and bushmen whose information he used in this neighbourhood, he viewed rolling back the boundaries of the unknown and advancing civilisation as the prerogative of the social elite. He never forgave New Zealand for the fact that in his bid to record the first ascent of Mt Cook he was forestalled by a group of colonials of the labouring class.

As to the question of the utility of the thing, it *does* matter, and the utility may be found in knowledge. As I grew older, the notion that I might contribute to knowledge became increasingly important; it concerned me that the knowledge that I had acquired with so much effort might disappear with me, that it might not be passed on. Naturally a good deal of it was not the sort of thing that can be recorded on a map or in a fieldbook, but rather was the practical knowledge of the hand or the eye, skills that cannot be expressed in words. Yet I wished to record on paper what could be preserved. I do not pretend that I did what I did in the hope that it would be useful for others, though certainly the knowledge I gathered was of use to me. What I would say is that I was glad to identify a respectable reason for doing what I was good at.

The realisation gradually dawned in me that it was the desire for knowledge, or discovery, if you will, that I shared with men like Mueller and Roberts. For them it was the goal of setting Westland down on the map in its entirety that mattered, not the possible rewards that might flow from it. It was a goal that arose as much from the satisfaction they found in travelling the country as from their professional training. In me that understanding crystallised more slowly; I had been largely unaware of the knowledge that was accumulating in my head, loose and jumbled up, like a box of newspaper clippings and sawdust that the first good gust of wind will blow to the four quarters.

AV: What is useful for the doer may not be useful for society, and vice–versa. Does society care about the reasons things that turn out to be useful are done? As long as somebody does them – even apparently absurd tasks such as mapping the vertical terrain of South Westland – the motives are likely to be irrelevant for those who come after.

CD: Perhaps for those who come after they matter little; for the individual and those who know him their significance is considerable. It is motivation that determines the manner in which the activity is carried out, and manner influences much. Consider, for example, Dr Julius von Haast, provincial bombast and misappropriator of the deeds of others

AV [*laughing*]: You really didn't like him, did you?

CD: The man was a manipulator. He was pleasant enough and could be helpful, but always with an eye on the main chance. Dr Haast enjoyed being a big fish in the provincial pond; nor was he tardy in eating small fry to grow even bigger. In the end, neither the land nor his companions mattered greatly for Haast: they were merely there to provide material for his ladder to fame and fortune.

AV: Roberts once said, Charlie, that you are a good hater as well as a good friend.

CD: "Be it mine to love my friend, but against the enemy, hateful indeed", says Pindar. But no, in all seriousness, if I despised him it was for a selfishness and mediocrity of which the diggers to whom he condescended would have been ashamed. As an explorer I took an interest in the naming of geographical features, as you may imagine. Well, friend Haast would dash about the country in a frenzy of naming. He named mountain ranges and rivers and streams and lakes and bogs after eminent scientists and other notables, English–speaking and German–speaking alike, and then he would write to the dignitaries in question, informing them of the way he,

Julius von Haast, had honoured them. Darwin, Tyndall, Hooker, Huxley, and all those others whose names I cannot remember or pronounce: he appealed to their vanity, and being human they liked it, so when the time came they did what they could to advance the interests of this respectful and helpful colonial. This was how Haast was able to work his way into the innermost circles of science, leaving behind on the maps of Canterbury and Westland a record of his wiles. An accomplished udder–squeezer if ever there was one, was our distinguished Dr Haast. So, yes, there comes a point at which motives do matter, even in the acquisition of knowledge supposedly for its own sake.

AV: Which reminds me, didn't you once name a range Udder–Squeezer Range, with a Mt So–and–So, Crawley Saddle, Humbug Creek and the like? Was that all in honour of Haast, or was it merely coincidence they were right beside the Haast River? I see that an irritable explorer can be a dangerous enemy.

CD: I neither deny nor affirm the allegation. Haast was not the only member of that class. The world was and remains, I am sure, well populated with udder–squeezers. Besides, I was not allowed to retain my Udder–Squeezer Range: Roberts exercised the senior surveyor's authority and vetoed the name, so I was obliged to even the score in other ways.

AV: Charlie, although you say you wanted to pass on your knowledge, you didn't write much, and there are those who have cursed you for that. There are some fieldnotes and reports, which don't tell us a great deal, and that's just about it, except for a few surviving letters.

CD: Ah, I know. The thing is, I was no good at writing about myself; seldom could I take myself seriously enough for that. Then when I did make a serious attempt to write it was too late. Like many an enthusiastic reader, I assumed that being able to appreciate a good book would be enough to make me a good writer, and was too easily discouraged when I discovered otherwise. Survey field reports are not a highly developed literary form, requiring gifts for neither self–portrayal nor deep analysis. All the same, Roberts habitually instructed us to 'pile on the agony', as he put it. The public liked it, he said, and a record of derring–do would make it easier to get funds for the following year's fieldwork.

AV: Roberts was a shrewd man who understood the public. He was tapping a vein that we tend to think of as strictly contemporary: the longing for vicarious excitement, for hardship and suffering experienced from the comfort of an armchair, thrills to take us out of the tedium and monotony of our daily lives. Vicarious excitement is a big industry these days, with countless individuals making a living from agony and drama piled on thick. Adventurers go in their hundreds on expeditions to the South Pole or the Himalaya and, if they manage to come back, inevitably write books about it, usually dwelling in gory detail on the dangers, the risks taken, the accidents, fatalities, disappearances, cases of insanity. There are those who have made a living from breaking a leg in the mountains and being left for dead, who rank staying alive as their greatest accomplishment. And their readers are encouraged to think this is what it means to be a hero: tough, fearless, more than a bit thick – rather like the agony they pile on, really. Then the readers go out in imitation, and some of them don't come back. Those who do survive, but with bits missing, become inspirational speakers at management seminars, giving lectures on You Don't Need All Your Body Parts to Succeed. It's a good message, to be sure, though advice on how to keep yourself in one piece would be better. They imagine all you need for success is cockiness and adrenalin.

CD: Adrenalin? It is an effort to keep up with the modern terminology. What is it, some kind of hair tonic?'

AV: Well, it certainly can make your hair stand on end. More like a drug, really. It gets into the blood and makes people stupid.

CD: Ah, now I'm with you. In Scotland they call it whisky. The British navy had a tradition of issuing rum for the same purpose.

AV: And the Russian army dispensed vodka. Yes, a bit like that. People get worked up, lose their reason and then do things that no one in their right mind would do. When they recover their senses they are in awe of what they have done and so feel compelled to write about it. There are library shelves full of the products of adrenalin. As a member of one of Shackleton's expeditions observed, if you are counting on the proceeds of the book to finance this expedition or the next, a proper amount of suffering is obligatory. When the public pays to watch gladiators, they can't just sit down in the middle of the Colosseum and have a picnic.

Although adrenalin, blood and suffering may make for a good read, it seems to me that there is a big difference between a successful book and a successful expedition. I like to think that a successful expedition needs other things, such as a clear intellect, self–discipline, sound judgement, good concentration and a sense of humour; and I am convinced that the best expeditions are precisely those on which nothing happens: no mistakes, no excessive hardship, no accidents; everything done capably and without fuss.

CD: Perhaps you're right. The *Iliad* is great literature, and I still carry my copy about with me, but I would just as soon have missed the siege of Troy. The leadership there sure didn't show much in the way of intelligence, humour or organisational ability.

AV: No need to go so far afield for examples either. That is what makes your exploration of this country impressive Charlie: all those rivers and mountain ranges travelled, from the Cascade Valley to Hokitika, and all done without fuss, competently, unhurriedly, all the time getting to know the landscape and responding to it. No heroics, no more than the shortest of spurts of adrenalin. You stayed alive, and while you did not exactly tell the tale, at least you had plenty of stories you might have told. I'm glad that the Royal Geographic Society got around to awarding you a medal.

CD [*self–consciously*]: Harper organised that. He was a man with connections. And while it made me feel silly at the time, I confess it gave me satisfaction. Even hermits, it would appear, crave a little recognition, a modicum of respect, especially from those with some understanding of what they have done.

AV: Sprezzatura.

CD: I beg your pardon? Is that some sort of singing instruction?

AV: Sprezzatura. Baldesar Castiglione formulated the idea when describing the perfect courtier during the 1520s. He meant something like nonchalance, the ability to do the most difficult things yet make them seem easy, as if you are not even raising a sweat. True art is the art that does not seem art; it appears effortless, and so it looks to the hoi polloi as if it could be done by any man or his dog. The cognoscenti, however, appreciate the amount of practice and skill required to make the achievement seem effortless, the amount of effort that lies behind a truly polished and graceful performance. When perfect performance has become routine it is pointless as well as ungracious to brag. Aristocratic cool – that's sprezzatura. The word is Italian, but the ideal is found everywhere: Renaissance Europe, ancient China, contemporary New Zealand.

I have to admit that it wins me every time. Meng Chih Fan comes to mind, who in 484 BC, when the army of the state of Lu was routed and was streaming back inside the city walls, stayed behind to fight a rearguard action. At the last moment, as he finally entered the city gate, he spurred his mount forward, commenting that he hadn't intended to lag behind; it was just that he couldn't get his horse to go faster. And Athol Whimp in 1996, returning to the Grand Plateau after his solo ascent of the Balfour Face of Mt Tasman; he had to be interrogated before he would even admit what he had done. Castiglione would have admired both the coolness of the deeds and modesty that followed them.

CD: "A grace beyond the reach of art", eh. Well, I have read Pope's line often enough, without ever thinking that it might apply to me. Somehow it is difficult for a man to convince himself that grace or art has anything much to do with pushing his way through scrub and clambering over rocks, wearing boots a beggar would not accept, with moss in his hair and a belly so empty you could fit it to a set of pipes and play a lively rendition of 'Loch Lomond'. I suppose it makes sense. But just now you mentioned the vulgar notion that even a dog may achieve sprezzatura. Well, let me tell you about my dog Topsy; if ever there was a dog with sprezzatura, it was she.

AV: Tospy? Would that be Topsy, the Lady of the Lake?

CD [*very pleased*]: Aye, the very same. Lake Topsy, near the Moeraki River. I named it for her because I wanted her contribution to be remembered. In many respects she was a better explorer than I and she deserves some credit. She taught me a thing or two; not only how to be content under bad conditions, or the art of living off the land, but also about route–finding through hard country.

When we came to a bluff by the river, or a gorge, I would sit down for a quiet smoke while Topsy went ahead to reconnoitre. She would scout the terrain so carefully and with such enjoyment that she could not wag her tail fast enough. In due course she would return, give me time to put on my swag, and lead off. If she followed the river I knew there would be a way through; if she started climbing away from the river I knew that going high would be the only way past the obstacle. Of course, it took me a while to learn this. A man likes to think he is smarter than a dog, especially when it comes to avoiding unnecessary effort. Well, on those occasions when I questioned her ability she never took umbrage. If I insisted on trying the river when she said we must go high, she simply shrugged her shoulders and curled up for a nap until I returned. She never said I told you so, or rubbed my nose in my mistakes; at most she would allow herself a superior smile and then trot off, with me behind her in my proper place. She was the most nonchalant and graceful aristocrat of a mongrel you could ever imagine.

AV: So we should aspire to doggish ease and enthusiasm, eh, and lollop around the hills with our tongues hanging out? I don't think Castiglione would approve. Charlie, it is so dark now that it is becoming hard to hear let alone see you. Were anyone to come along they would think I'm talking to myself and crazy. Thank you for staying with me. I know you were never a great talker, so I hope you don't mind having been made to chatter on.

CD: The pleasure has been mine. The dead get so little opportunity to talk that it would be churlish to complain. One learns to be thankful for small mercies. At least you were not tempted to put a tam–o–shanter on my head and give me a false Scotch accent.

A little later I went through the darkness to the river, walking out to the middle of the swingbridge to look at the night. A breeze rose from the motion of the water, flowing with it down the valley and stirring the trees along the bank. It was fresh and alive. Overhead the sky was full of stars. The radiant edge of the galaxy spanned the valley, bridging with star clusters and constellations the space between one range and the other. Light that had been travelling for hundreds of millions of years fell around me like fine rain. It fell beyond the mountains and on the forest trees whose leaves trembled on the night wind. Starlight foamed in the rushing river beneath me, washed together with water from the Ruera and Strauchon Valleys, from Copland Pass and the northern slopes of Mt Sefton. Invisibly the river's current carved rocks and planed banks as it disappeared into darkness and the gorge below, on its way to join the Karangarua River in its final passage to the sea.

CHAPTER TWELVE

For whom will you do it?
Who will you get to listen to you?
– Ssu–ma Ch'ien, *Letter to Jen Shao–ch'ing*

Ranges grow and clouds gather, rocks break and rivers carry the silt to the sea. Mountains are processes, not fixed entities, yet in their slow change there is time enough for us to do some of what we dream. Moments come when all the elements converge, when mental clarity and stillness come together with physical fitness, when conditions in the mountains are favourable and a wind blowing from the right direction prompts us to venture out confidently.

For years I had been biding my time, storing in my mind the idea of climbing the full west ridge of Mt Tasman, from the coastal plain to its summit on the Main Divide. In a single journey I would traverse all the zones of vegetation and alpine terrain that Westland compresses in its abrupt rise from the sea to permanent ice. Starting at 160 metres above sea level, at the edge of the Fox River flats, the ridge ends eighteen kilometres later on Mt Tasman's ice–cap at an altitude of 3497 metres. In straightforward terms this makes it the longest climb possible in New Zealand.

Its scale, variety, scenery and solitude set the west ridge of Tasman apart, but there is another feature that also makes it special: there is a bus stop right at the beginning of the climb. No long approach march here! On the morning of 6 December 1999, that is where the southbound bus drops me off, by the DoC sign marking the start of the Mt Fox track, one kilometre past the Fox River Bridge.

The ascent starts at the road edge. I climb a bank, push through wineberry bushes and enter rainforest so dark that my eyes need time to adjust; in the space of ten or twelve paces the world is transformed from the light and openness of farmland and river flats to a forest dense with green, shadow and coolness, where even the air seems palpable. There is

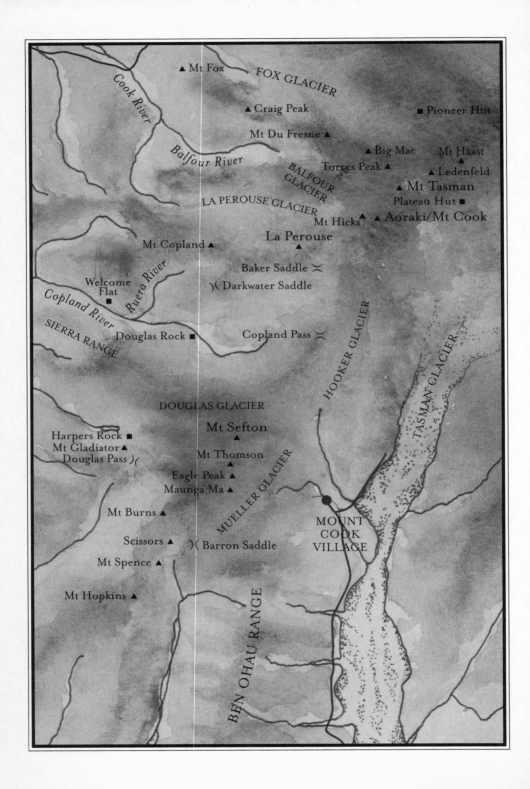

not the faintest movement in the leaves, which even in the dimness of the forest canopy scatter silver light from yesterday's raindrops. Sound from the highway is muffled; already the bitumen and its users are remote. Under the trees there is a second sign, this one warning that the track to Mt Fox is steep and poorly formed.

The track *is* steep. It offers only a few minutes in which to prepare myself before it turns sharply upward through thick forest festooned with ferns and kiekie, over roots and mud that make the going slippery. In no time I am sweating profusely, despite the coolness of the morning. I avoid hauling myself up on the vegetation and minimise jerky movements, trying to achieve the steady rhythm that will enable me to keep on going. The trees are tall, imposing, their trunks covered with epiphytes; the understorey is lush and varied. It is impossible not to respond to the forest's richness and it distracts me from the effort I am making. Already I am glad that I have had to wait for four days with the Millers at Docherty Creek for the right weather for my undertaking; it has given me time to climb some of the tracks around Franz Josef Glacier and improve my fitness. The trees become smaller, but when I enter the subalpine zone the undergrowth becomes more prolific rather than sparser, as stunted trees and shrubs, unsure of who is what, compete for space. Mountain neinei, hakeke, tupare and groundsel jostle each other and push in on the track, which struggles to hold its own. Soon, however, it emerges from the thickets, and there, without even a proper bump on the ridge to call its own, is the trig station labelled Mt Fox. It was established under the direction of George Roberts during the 1870s. The track I have climbed is marked as a blazed route on the 1896 sketch map of the Fox basin based on Charlie Douglas' field-work.

The coastal plain is now 900 metres below. The sky is deep blue and enormous, the plain and ocean free of cloud; only the crest of the range, not far above me, is hidden from view, and the seaward face of the ranges to the south. Slowly I continue the ascent along the crest of the ridge. Soon there is little other than turpentine scrub, stunted celery pine, and persistent hebes growing among snow tussocks. A few ourisia in bloom are the only flowers visible. Where the ridge levels off briefly there are some small tarns, while far below on the left the white ice of the Fox Glacier fills its deep valley: it will be another two days before I reach its head.

Suddenly I catch sight of movement on the ridge not far above me. A solitary figure descends, and even from a distance I can see that this a happy man. He has a spring in his stride and when we meet his enthusiasm is infectious: he is full of the joy of his morning. Leaving Fox township early and travelling light, he had climbed through the cloud to the first eminence on the range and there sat for three hours enjoying the scenery being made and unmade around him. In the space of a few minutes Mark and I discover that we have a number of mutual friends, as well as a shared love of forests. Then we shake hands and he continues down, still radiating happiness, while I, radiating more heat than light, carry on into the cloud to reach Point 1345, not long before vacated by my new–found friend.

When the cloud rolls away momentarily it reveals a landscape very different from the one up which I have been struggling. Ahead, the undulating crest of the range disappears into cloud banks that will continue to rise all day out of the Cook and Balfour Valleys on my right, pushed up by a persistent southerly breeze. The slopes up which the cloud drifts, like the crest of the range itself, are covered by tussock herbfields; only in sheltered hollows among the boulders do a few shrubs manage to survive. As I proceed along the range the breeze is pleasantly cool; the cloud is no cause for concern, even when visibility is reduced to fifty metres. On my left the range falls steeply 1000 metres down to the Fox Glacier, but so as long as I remember which is left and which is right there is little likelihood of going astray. Only when a rock outcrop on the crest blocks progress do I have to backtrack and detour a little.

The journey takes on a pleasant, vaguely forlorn quality as I step along the breezy cloud–swept ridge, on one side are grassy slopes dotted with sombre tarns and raked by mist, on the other the void into which the cloud spills and disappears. It is difficult to decide whether the world is ending or just beginning. All it needs for a classic romantic scene is an agitated Schiller or Wordsworth to emerge from the mist, scribbling poetry with furrowed brow.

But the cloud *does* cause a problem. As usual in cloud or mist, I overestimate the distance I have covered. I seldom have trouble with direction, it is just that I tend to confuse how far I would like to have come with the distance actually travelled; time and space pass more quickly in my head than in reality. When I think I must be nearing Craig Peak – at an altitude of 1914 metres the first summit of any significance, which I have set as my goal for the day – a break in the cloud enables me to fix my position, and to my chagrin discover that there is still a good two kilometres to go.

The range narrows and climbs higher; I leave behind the tussock slopes, the ground becomes bare and rocky. The first snowdrifts appear, small and few in number, for once again it has been a winter of meagre snowfalls, at least on the lower ranges. There are fresh chamois tracks across the drifts, some of them heading in the direction I am taking, so it appears that I will have company along the way. Now Craig Peak is close at hand, across a rocky basin traversed by the chamois, with patches of grass on its final ridge. With any luck this, the upper limit of the vegetation, will provide me with a comfortable sleeping place.

The grass is soft and springy, perfect for a night out, though the location is terribly exposed to the weather. As I cook my dinner, I keep a wary eye on black rain clouds depositing their burden in the Cook and Copland Valleys and seemingly moving in my direction. As the sun begins to set, however, the clouds dissolve. Walking fifty metres around a corner, I am amazed by the sight of the high peaks – Tasman, Cook, La Perouse and Sefton – so close and so high. I know them well, yet once again I am astonished to see how massive they are and how far they rise above me.

Dawn breaks white with frost. My sleeping–bag and pack are barely distinguishable from the surrounding grass and rocks. The night has been my first experiment with a new lightweight sleeping–bag and I am glad to have passed the night warmly, even though it required wearing all the clothing I have with me. But once day has broken there is no temptation to linger. So far everything has gone well and I am moderately pleased with my performance: I am more or less on schedule and without too many aches and pains, despite yesterday's long climb and what feels like a heavy load; the route has been as easy as I'd hoped; and I have been correct in my assessment of the weather. It is today, however, that represents the big unknown. I have examined the range between Sam Peak and Mt Du Fresne from the air and confirmed what the contour map plainly indicates: that the range turns into a series of rock towers and spires about one and a half kilometres long, squeezed between the Balfour Glacier to the south and the Mascarin Glacier to the north. It looked feasible from the air, but I have not heard of anyone passing this way before. In an aeroplane it is easy to be deceived.

By seven–thirty I am on top of Craig Peak. While the sky overhead is clear, the lower ranges are hidden in dark cloud. Mts Tasman and Cook rise, huge and intimidating, between me and the morning sun, which lights up plumes of powder snow blowing from their summits on a strong southerly wind. On Craig Peak the southerly drift is light, yet already it is lifting cloud out of the Balfour Valley and pushing it across my range. I hope that will cause no route–finding problems.

At any rate, the route past Sam Peak is clear. I descend small bluffs and snow slopes to reach a level expanse of dark brown stone, devoid of vegetation except for a profusion of mountain buttercups which lift their yellow flowers just above the ground and frame them with bright green leaves. Sidling along below the main ridge, across steep scree and snow, I reach the basin below Sam Peak where McKenna Creek, an old prospectors' route, begins its descent to the Balfour Valley. Here too it is only the buttercups that bring the stones to life; the few tufts of grass and other plants huddling miserably in rocky crevices make little contribution. The small stream gurgling down over the stones to form McKenna Creek is music to my ears, for already I am very thirsty, my water bottles are empty, and I have been anxious at the possibility of not finding anything to drink before the serious climbing of the day begins. In the stream's presence I rest, enjoying its sound and motion, quenching my thirst leisurely and thoroughly before setting off once more.

As I climb out of the basin the terrain changes again. The range narrows to a single ridge, on which stunted vegetation manages to re–establish a presence, but the ridge itself seems to lack both the determination of the plants and their ability to hold the ground together. Slumps in the underlying rocks and ancient moraines have dissected it so badly that climbing through the cloud I find it difficult to judge which is the main crest. In places the ridge resembles an autumn glacier, so sharply cut are its crevasses of gravel, at the bottom of which lie sorry and bewildered–looking plants. However, my chamois friends have already passed this way, so when unsure of which way to go I look for their hoofprints in the soil.

It is well into the morning when I reach the top of a broad rise, to see a line of rock towers disappearing into the mist ahead and blocking further progress along the crest of the range. The chamois tracks head to the left of these obstacles, so that is the direction I take. A steep bluff leads down to nasty gullies filled with rubble. These do not appear to have troubled my four–footed guides, but I find the loose rock unnerving. I take out my light abseil rope and pass it round a bollard to use as a safety line. When I pull it down behind me it has already worked itself free and is cut almost in half by a rock that falls down onto it. This is not an auspicious start to the ropework and leaves me ill–equipped for whatever may follow. But now a brief clearance of the cloud enables me to see that by descending a little further to a snow slope, a short sidle will enable me to climb up a steep but easy slope back to the crest of the range. Tired, and moving slowly, eventually I haul myself up onto a broad rocky summit which must be what the map labels Crozet Peak. It is a good place for a badly needed rest.

The way ahead remains lost in cloud. In a way this is an advantage, for not being able to see how many towers and pinnacles I have to nego-tiate prevents me from worrying about them; I have to concentrate on what lies immediately in front of me and solve each problem as it confronts me from the mist. From the top of Crozet Peak a snow shoulder leads me to the Balfour side of the range, and while this is steeper than the northern slope, it is free of loose rock, for any surface less than vertical is covered by a heavy layer of spring snow. It is on this side that I sidle most of the obstacles that continue to rise up out of the mist during the afternoon. As I top a rise on the crest of the range there is a sharp warning whistle below me: a chamois buck tells his family to get out of the way of my clumsy feet. The doe speeds off down a gully, her young kid almost under her legs in its panic, an elder sibling close behind and the buck bringing up the rear. When I follow I try to be careful with loose stones, and return as soon as I can to the ridge crest.

Now the range climbs a little, rising to a prominent peak which, I will learn later, though unnamed is higher than Crozet Peak. As I reach its summit the mist parts again, giving a brief glimpse of what is still to come. I have only an approximate idea where I am. Beyond the towers at my feet, a steep and slender snowy peak emerges from the cloud – I guess it is Mt Du Fresne, but cannot be sure – while far behind, and so much higher that I catch my breath, is the unmistakable summit of Tasman. Slowly, very slowly, I continue, keeping to the snow as much as possible, stopping frequently to sip water, rest and spy out the way forward. I weave my way around more pinnacles. The slopes above the Balfour Glacier are beginning to feel airy; the range seems to be working itself up to something. Surely it can only be Mt Du Fresne? A long snow slope eventually brings me to a summit. Is this it? I hope so, for I am tired.

Through the cloud I can make out a broad glacial slope ahead, but because the mist distorts the distance cannot tell how far away it is. There seem to be more rock towers below me. As I set off down the rocks there is another loud whistle; again the chamois family darts out from under my feet and leaps away down a gully to the snow slopes below. All day, unconsciously, I have been herding them along the range, and they have had enough. It is the last I see of them. The cloud rolls back a little, finally revealing that I have indeed reached the point where the ridge of rock towers merges with the broad ridge of permanent ice and snow that forms the southern edge of the Fox Glacier. For one last time I am able follow the chamois, since as usual they have picked the best route down to the snow. It is there that the parting of our ways occurs: they are already on their way back down to slopes beside the Mascarin Glacier, while I turn uphill, in the direction of the ridge leading towards Big Mac, Mt Torres and Mt Tasman.

The snow is slush in which I sink to my knees. Two hundred metres of it is enough. It is six–thirty and I have been on the move for twelve hours. The goal I have set for the day, Big Mac, is still a couple of kilometres further along the ridge and 400 metres higher. If I continue climbing, I will become extremely tired, get wet feet and may not find anywhere off the snow to camp. Therefore it would be wiser to camp here, on the rocks, and continue the climb in the morning, when, with any luck, the surface will be firm with frost. It is an easy decision to make.

Nearby, above a windscoop on the Fox side of the ridge, is a ledge covered with loose rock that I can rearrange to make a sleeping platform. When I unpack I discover another good reason for staying where I am: somehow, during the day, in the course of emptying and restowing my pack, I have managed to lose my sleeping–bag. How is it possible? In fluent Irish I curse myself: fuckin' eejit!

As the sun sets, much of the cloud disappears. Across the head of

Balfour Valley the high peaks – Tasman, Cook, Dampier, Hicks and La Perouse – compete for light; they catch the rays of the sinking sun and hold them, releasing them only grudgingly. Lesser peaks like Magellan and Drake rise sharp and savage; they look very close in the encroaching shadow of night.

Even without a sleeping–bag my ledge is quite comfortable; there is room to turn, and with all my clothes and parka on the cold of the night is not unpleasant, let alone unbearable. For long periods I manage to sleep rather than lie awake looking at my watch and urging on the minutes. In the moonless sky the stars shine brilliantly as they gravitate slowly towards the western horizon. Far below, on the coastal plain, two lights are visible along the road to Gillespies Beach. Towards dawn, out at sea, powerful lights indicate the presence of fishing boats.

With the first hint of morning I am on my way. Although there has been a hard frost and the surface is crisp, it is a strange sullen dawn that leaves the coast clouded over and the high peaks hidden from view. No sooner do I reach the crest of the first rise in the ridge above my camp, from where Big Mac is visible, then dark cloud once more begins to roll in from the Balfour Valley, pushed along by the steady southerly airstream. It does not worry me greatly, since at this point navigation should not be a problem; all I have to do is keep near the crest of the ridge as I climb. Should the weather deteriorate, however, it would be a concern, for the Fox Neve is not a friendly place in bad weather, particularly for a lone traveller.

Big Mac stops me in my tracks. I have been unsure whether it will be possible to traverse high around it; Alex Miller did give me advice about the best option, but I have forgotten what he said. Now, from below its summit block, which leans over the Balfour like the Tower of Pisa, I can see that the Balfour side is too steep to be attractive. While climbing the rocks of the summit ridge and then descending on the far side seems possible, it is not a choice for which I feel in the mood. The only option that remains, then, is to descend the northern slope, losing the 400 metres height I have gained this morning, all the way to the lower Abel Janszoon Glacier, and follow it in the direction of Katies Col and the beginning of the Torres–Tasman traverse.

By the time I have reached the Abel Janszoon Glacier – the stream of the Fox Glacier that drains the foot of Mt Tasman itself – a change in strategy has worked itself out. From where I am now it will be late morning before I am able to begin climbing Mt Torres, yet the limited knowledge I have of the Torres–Tasman traverse centres on the fact that it is a long, long way. I have also been a little anxious at the thought of climbing Mt Tasman with all the baggage I am carrying and have been toying with the idea of dumping some of my stuff near Katies Col, to be picked up on the way down. But that type of strategy rarely works out and in this case would require me to traverse Mt Torres twice. What is more, I am feeling dehydrated and in serious need of not just one but a whole series of drinks. Two hours away, near the centre of the Fox Glacier, is Pioneer Hut, where I will be able to get all the drinks I crave, have a leisurely afternoon and relatively comfortable night, and then return to my task early in the morning, travelling light, with plenty of time up my sleeve. It is not difficult to reach a decision and it proves to be one of the best I have made.

Before heading for the hut, however, I continue up the Abel Janszoon Glacier, past Katies Col, until directly below the summits of Torres and Tasman. A casual glance confirms that conditions are extremely icy: the rock buttresses of both peaks are heavily sheathed in a wintry layer of white. Conditions on the glacier, on the other hand, are excellent; the slopes roll away unbroken, with scarcely a crevasse to be seen under the spring snow. With its surface frozen after the cold night, the glacier offers almost carefree travelling. On the trek over to Pioneer Hut I have little to grumble about: high cloud filters the sun, the surface remains firm and the crevasses are few and easy to spot. All that detracts from my holiday mood is a slight ache in my shoulders and my nagging thirst.

Pioneer Hut itself is brand new, erected only seven months previously, the fourth in the series. Pioneer I, built nearby at the end of the Pioneer Ridge, was destroyed by rockfall. Pioneer II, constructed a kilometre away below Mt Alack, was destroyed by DoC officers when the rock on which it was built started to fall to bits. Pioneer III, which occupied the same site as its successor, was a victim of faulty foundations which made it buckle at the knees when pushed by the weight of winter snow. The newness of Pioneer IV means that it lacks the sordidness typical of huts above the snowline, while the company makes it better still. After a few hours of conversation, Dave Chowdhury and Brendan Kane seem old friends, though this is the first time we have met; and it proves the same with Rob Kirkwood and Paula Marshall when they return to the hut from their climb. There is none of the edgy competitiveness that sometimes gets into the water supply of mountain huts and corrodes climbers from the inside. It is a relaxed, well–watered, less solitary traveller who turns in that evening.

December 9 does not start well. I have set the alarm on my new watch for three in the afternoon instead of three in the morning, and by the time I wake up all the other parties have already set off on their various expeditions. But I will not make many more mistakes today. At a quarter to four, fifteen minutes after getting up, I am on my way, searching by torch-light for my tracks of the previous day. Near the hut they have largely been obliterated by the sun. After a couple of false leads, however, I find my way through the breaks in the ice below the hut and it becomes easier. Again the surface is crisp with frost, providing quick travelling. Soon I reach the broken section of the Abel Janszoon Glacier. By climbing slightly as I veer to the right, I strike a good way through: I ascend a deep trough between tall seracs, cross several wide crevasses whose depths are darker than the night around me, skirt around the glacial bulge that follows, then find I can descend directly to the foot of the slope that leads up to Katies Col, not far from where I descended from Big Mac yesterday. It is now light enough to put away my torch. Steadily, almost without effort thanks to my light load, I climb the slope, to arrive on the col at around six o'clock. I am feeling very relaxed, at ease in what I am doing.

The Balfour side of the col looks hostile. Black cloud fills the valley, churning on a cold dawn wind and climbing the ice cliffs below me. Across the valley, dwarfing Magellan and Drake, rise the massive faces of Cook, Dampier and Hicks, dark and menacing; they are so close that I feel walled in by mountain ramparts. Once over the col I climb upwards to the left on steep snow, making for the rock rib that will take me up onto the main west ridge of Torres. As I climb, the snow becomes harder and turns to ice, hard ice, on which only the front four points of my crampons find purchase. The slope becomes a little steeper. Doubt creeps in: here I am, barely off the deck, yet feeling nervous; what am I getting myself into? The hard ice continues, and with it my discomfort, on and on, up towards the crest of the rib. The rib crest turns out to be ice too, masked here and there with powdery snow. But as I ascend my confidence increases; climbing on front points with ice–axe in one hand and ice–hammer in the other, the tip of their picks in the surface for support, begins to feel all right. By the time I reach the main ridge I have ceased to worry about ice, rock, or the space below my feet; my attention is absorbed wholly by movement.

I have moved from shadow to sun; perhaps that makes a difference, or maybe it is the fact that on the ridge it is easier to see that I'm making progress than when climbing the ice slope. But the ridge is extremely narrow, twisting and turning as it snakes towards the summit of Mt Torres. First comes a sharp curve of ice, then it turns a corner over rock towers, then another corner and more ice. A treacherous cover of recently fallen snow lies over every feature, wet and sticky on the northern side of the ridge, flaky and powdery on the southern side, adhering uncertainly to the ice and lying thickly over the rocks. Every step needs care and precision. I concentrate on each obstacle as I come to it, refusing to be distracted by what may or may not lie ahead. Seen from afar, difficulties tend to look intimidating, yet when one gets up close a solution often presents itself. So it is here: round a corner and a connecting section of ridge crosses what a moment earlier looked like space; rock pinnacles that rise vertically in the distance turn out to be easy, with plenty of holds. Be careful: be patient: relax: keep it smooth: steady: don't try to hurry. A line of snow arcs sharply upward and I am on the summit of Mt Torres, 3160 metres above sea level, exactly 3000 metres above my starting point on the West Coast highway. It is about ten–thirty in the morning and Mt Tasman is only another 337 metres higher.

There is no room to sit down and the ice is too steep even to rest standing, so I move on, down the far side of the sharp summit pyramid, then up again over snow–covered rock towers, and abruptly down another snow crest to the gap between Torres and Tasman. Now there is a lot more than 337 metres to go: about 450, in fact. What is more, those will be the most difficult of the whole journey. From where I stand a ridge of green ice rises steeply to an even steeper buttress of rock; that is to say, I know there usually is a buttress of rock hereabouts, but now everything is covered in thick bulges and large feathers of ice, the same pale green and white as the slopes below.

Well, okay, but first I need a rest, something to drink, and a few minutes respite from the sun. Below the gap, on its southern side, is a yawning bergschrund with an overhanging upper lip that casts its shadow on a flat surface below it. It is well worth a brief wade through knee–deep snow to get there: I can sit on my pack, stretch out my legs, encourage the blood to return to toes that are numb from kicking crampon points into the mountain, and force down some food. Despite my hunger, eating is an effort. My throat is so dry that the only way I can swallow is to mix food with snow and wash it down with a few mouthfuls of water from my bottle. In the shadow of the ice cliff it is pleasantly cool, but I do not sit too closely under it: from directly below, the ice looks big and threatening.

An hour's rest and I am ready to move on. The ice slope to the base of the rock rises at a sharp angle and is longer than it appears from below. As I climb, I move leftward, heading for a shallow gully that will take me to where the rocks are shortest, near where the ridge begins to form again. There is wet snow lying on the steep ice, and grooves marking the tracks of avalanches triggered by ice debris falling from the vertical wall above. The warm sun seems to be doing its best to bring down more debris, so I move quickly, stopping only to catch my breath and rest my calves.

Here, near its left–hand edge, the rock buttress is not high; the problem is that the ice bulges covering it are overhanging and dripping with water. The edge itself, overlooking the Abel Janszoon Face, is a vertical array of long ice feathers fastened to the rock by the south wind; although less steep, they are also less stable than the bulges forming frozen cascades on the right. Moving right a few steps, I climb to the base of a small rock overhang split by a vertical crack and belabour the ice above it with my hammer. Slabs, icicles, sheets of ice rain down. When I tire I climb down to some ice–free rocks at the top of the gully, rest, then return to my defrosting. As I try to climb the rock I uncover, I have to face up to the knowledge I have been avoiding: the rock is the wrong shape, with nothing to hold onto to pull myself past the overhang. So I have another rest, hack away a bit more, then try a slightly different manoeuvre to get up the rock. Still no go. Maybe those ice feathers to the left would be a better a option after all? But no, they are still just as dangerous as before.

I lose track of time. Two hours pass, maybe more. Still, I remain cool, thinking things through and calmly pursuing the options. One option I do leave untried, for it holds no appeal at all, is going back down the ice slope below and trying to climb on the right of the buttress. With the ice covering the rock dripping continuously in the afternoon sun, it seems a risky proposition. The problem is, I have exhausted all the possibilities where I am, so what am I to do? From my resting spot I notice some easy–looking rocks that lead off to the right, a few metres below me, to a slight nose of rock that blocks the view of what comes next. It is worth a try. Minutes later I am around the corner and above me rises a narrow line of steep red slabs, surprisingly free of ice. So big and secure are the handholds that I am able to reach the top of the buttress with my pulse thudding calmly rather than racing. Above, the final ridge of ice curves towards the summit. Between us no obstacle remains.

Well, nothing except human frailty, that is, for mental and physical effort have taken their toll. Although its angle is now easy, the surface of the ridge is a treacherous mixture of hard ice and wet powder snow that balls up my crampons. Besides, from the summit it will still be a long way home, and it is on homeward journeys that most errors and accidents occur. I keep telling myself to be careful, to concentrate, that I must not relax yet. My rest stops become longer, the time lapses between them shorter. There is no temptation to hurry. As I reach the peak's western shoulder an Air Safaris twin engine Nomad approaches from the north and flies close by at my altitude; it appears to waggle its wings. It may be my old friend Richard Rayward flying it, so I give a wave. The aeroplane disappears in the direction of Baker Saddle, to reappear five minutes later and fly close by in the opposite direction. I wave again at the faces inside, then focus on what I am doing.

Where the ridge flattens I wallow briefly in wet powder snow, before ascending a slow curve of ice that levels off where it intersects two other ice ridges, one from the north and one from the south. This is the summit. It is five–thirty in the evening. Not counting the diversion to Pioneer Hut, from the road it has taken thirty–five hours of climbing time to get here. The air is warm and absolutely still; there is not even breeze enough to cool the sweat on my brow, which actually is quite heated. In the west the declining sun is reflected by the Tasman Sea, while nearer the cloud banks that troubled me earlier in the ascent still lie darkly against the lower ranges, hiding much of the coastal plain. The lower reaches of the range I have climbed – including Mt Du Fresne, Crozet Peak and Craig Peak – are barely visible, slight protuberances all but lost in an immensity of ocean, sky and cloud. But I know that somewhere down there, near the head of McKenna Creek, my chamois family is munching on the celmisia coming into bud; that further down the range, where mist combs through the rata trees, my footprints are fading as strand by strand the moss springs back from the pressure of my boots, just as on the neve the sun and frost will already be erasing every trace of my passage.

I take some photographs, then start down the north ridge. Five hours later, with night deepening around me, I climb the last slow rise of the Fox Glacier to Pioneer Hut. There is just enough light left to make out its silhouette. As I approach I am amazed to see a cluster of people standing outside in the darkness, waiting, I discover, to shake my hand, to welcome me back and express their delight at my safe return. Tears come to my eyes, but in the dark no one can see them. Yesterday I did not know Brendan, Dave, Ben, Paula, Rob, Glynis or Stephen; now I am moved by their concern and by their understanding of what the journey means to me. I will tell them more about it one day, for I know that even if I get caught up in details that convey more enthusiasm than information, they will just smile good naturedly and wait for me to get back to the story.

The next day we all go down the Fox Glacier to Chancellor Hut. From here the others fly out by helicopter, while Dave and I walk down the lower glacier and the road, to reach the highway one kilometre from my starting point. That evening, Rob and Paula take us all fishing for kahawai at Bruce Bay, where the Mahitahi River flows into the sea. It is a stormy night; a northwest wind whips up the breakers and rolls black cloud against the ranges. In the company of my friends, sitting by a big driftwood fire, I am content. Solitary experiences have enriched me, yet by sharing those experiences I become richer still, for the act of telling gives them a structure and depth they would otherwise lack. The telling, like the journey itself, is a process of discovery. Although in some ways the landscapes traversed differ, in the end each illuminates the other. Sometimes it appears as if putting experience into words calls for more courage than the experience itself; after all it requires a conviction that someone will listen and understand what we have to say. Since the evening at Bruce Bay I have that conviction.

SOURCES AND FURTHER READING

Chapter 1
Page 9 – Vilhjalmur Stefansson is quoted by Roland Huntford, *The Last Place on Earth: Scott and Amundsen's Race to the South Pole*, 2nd ed., The Modern Library, New York, 1999 (originally published as *Scott and Amundsen*, 1979), 172. The observation does not seem to occur anywhere in Stefansson's published works.

Chapter 2
Page 16 – Conrad Kain's autobiography, *Where the Clouds Can Go* (edited, with additional chapters, by J. Monroe Thorington) Charles T. Branford, Boston, 1954, unfortunately contains no account of his ascent either of Mt Thomson (with H. O. Frind) or Eagle Peak (with H. F. Wright). It does include material on Maunga Ma, of which he made the first ascent with Frind and Peter Graham.

Pages 17–18 – Shackleton's experience is discussed by Roland Huntford, *Shackleton*, Hodder and Stoughton, London, 1985, 695–97. In his own account of the *Endurance* expedition, *South*, William Heinemann, London, 1919, Shackleton has less to say than Huntford.

Page 18 – Hermann Buhl, *Nanga Parbat Pilgrimage*, trans. Hugh Merrick, 1962; rpt. Penguin, Harmondsworth, 1982, 400–01.

Page 19 – Greg Child, 'The Other Presence' (1989), rpt. in Child, *Mixed Emotions*, The Mountaineers, Seattle, 1993. Child discusses experiences other than his own, including those of Shackleton, Smythe and Messner. Those with a taste for enthusiastic explorations of esoterica such as this may enjoy Rob Schultheis, *Bone Games: Extreme Sports, Shamanism, Zen, and the Search for Transcendence*, 1984, rpt. Breakaway Books, New York, 1996.

Mountains as places of spiritual power are discussed by Mircea Eliade, *Shamanism: Archaic Techniques of Ecstasy*, Routledge and Kegan Paul, London, 1964, 264–74; and John Einarsen, ed., *The Sacred Mountains of Asia*, Shambala, London, 1995.

Chapter 3

Page 28 – K. A. Wodzicki, *Introduced Mammals of New Zealand: An Ecological and Economic Survey*, Dept. of Scientific and Industrial Research, Wellington, 1950, provides a useful discussion of the introduction of thar, chamois and deer into the Southern Alps.

Page 29 – On Fyfe and Graham, see John Haynes, *Piercing the Clouds*, Hazard Press, Christchurch, 1994, 74–82.

Page 31 – Gerhard Mueller's map of the Landsborough–Clarke basin and the accompanying report is in *Appendices to the Journal of the House of Representatives of New Zealand*, 1887, C–2, 12–13. Useful information on the history of the Landsborough Valley (and other parts of South Westland) is gathered by John Pascoe, *The Haast is in South Westland*, A. H. & A. W. Reed, Wellington, 1966.

Pages 34-35 – The only extant account of the journey by Docherty, Hassing and Spriggins is that by Hassing, in *Pages From the Memory Log of G. M. Hassing*, Southland Times, Invercargill, 1930, 32–35.

Page 35 – On the journey by Harper and Ruera Te Naihi see *Appendices to the Journal of the House of Representatives of New Zealand*, 1895, and A. P. Harper, *Pioneer Work in the Alps of New Zealand*, T. Fisher Unwin, London, 1896.

Chapter 4

Page 36 – Primo Levi, *The Truce: A Survivor's Journey Home From Auschwitz*, 1963, trans. Stuart Woolf, Vintage.

Chapter 5

Page 45 – P. R. May, *The West Coast Gold Rushes*, 2nd ed., Pegasus Press, Christchurch, 1967. May's book is an excellent source on early European exploration and settlement in Westland. Additional information is also available in the government reports included in *Appendices to the Journal of the House of Representatives*, especially those of the gold commissioners and provincial surveyors.

Pages 48-54 – The best sources on William Docherty are Heinrich Ferdinand von Haast, *The Life and Times of Sir Julius von Haast*, H. F. von Haast, Wellington, 1948; and A. C. and N. C. Begg, *Dusky Bay*, 2nd ed., Whitcombe and Tombs, Christchurch, 1968. Haast's biography includes a copy of his 1870 map. See also Andreas Reischek, *Yesterdays in Maoriland*, trans. H. E. L. Priday, 1930, rpt. Wilson and Horton, Auckland, 1970; and Hassing, *Pages From the Memory Log of G. M. Hassing.*

Page 49 – The historian is John Pascoe, *Great Days in New Zealand Exploration*, A. H. & A. W. Reed, Wellington, 1959, 128.

Chapter 6
Page 61 – There are a number of good translations of the *Inner Chapters* of Chuang Tzu (died c. 286 BC), including Burton Watson, *The Complete Works of Chuang Tzu*, Columbia U. P., New York, 1968; Gia–fu Feng and Jane English, *Chuang Tsu: Inner Chapters*, Wildwood House, London, 1974; Angus Graham, *Chuang–tzu*, George Allen & Unwin, London, 1981. In Chapter 4, 'In the World of Men', Chuang Tzu presents 'fasting of the mind' as a technique for staying alive in turbulent times, which entails mastery and elimination of emotions and anxieties that disturb inner harmony.

Page 63 – In ancient China the idea of eremitism as a matter of mental detachment rather than physical isolation owed much to Chuang Tzu, but perhaps its best known practitioners are the philosopher Chuang Tsun (also known as Yan Chün–p'ing; died c. AD 6) and the poet T'ao Ch'ien (also known as T'ao Yüan–ming; AD 365–427). I have written about this topic in 'Zhuang Zun: A Daoist Philosopher of the Late First Century BC', *Monumenta Serica*, vol. 38, 1988–89, 69–94; and *Men of the Cliffs and Caves: The Development of the Chinese Eremitic Tradition to the End of the Han Dynasty*, Chinese University of Hong Kong Press, Hong Kong, 1990. T'ao, one of China's greatest poets, wrote many poems about living in seclusion. His complete works have been translated into English by A. R. Davis, *T'ao Yüan–ming: His Works and Their Meaning*, Hong Kong University Press, Hong Kong, 1983.

Chapter 7

Page 72 – I prefer not to mention autobiographical accounts by living mountaineers. The tradition of celebrating Himalayan mountaineering suffering and disaster was raised to new literary levels by Maurice Herzog *Annapurna*, trans. Nea Morin and Janet Adam Smith, Cape, London, 1952, which became an influential model. The relation of Herzog's account to historical reality is examined by David Robert's, 'Rewriting Annapurna', *Climbing*, no. 173, Dec 1997– Feb 1998, 72–78. Accounts of the 1996 Everest disaster(s) include Jon Krakauer, *Into Thin Air: A Personal Account of the Mount Everest Disaster*, Random House, New York, 1997; and Anatoli Boukreev and G. Weston DeWalt, *The Climb: Tragic Ambitions on Everest*, St Martin's Press, New York, 1997. See also Colin Monteath, *Hall and Ball: Kiwi Mountaineers: From Mount Cook to Everest*, Hedgehog House, Christchurch, 1997. On K2, 1986 was a similarly disastrous year, the events of which are narrated by Jim Curran, *K2: Triumph and Tragedy*, The Mountaineers, Seattle, 1987, also Kurt Diemberger, *The Endless Knot: K2. Mountain of Dreams and Destiny*, Grafton Books, London, 1991. An new twist to this fascination with disasters was provided by the 1999 American expedition to find the bodies of George Mallory and Charles Irvine, who disappeared in 1927 while attempting the North Ridge of Mt Everest. Despite my predisposition to loathe the enterprise and distaste for the way photographs of Mallory's mummified body were given wide circulation (including a television documentary, with close–ups), I was compelled to conclude that the climbers involved were decent, sensitive individuals. See Jochen Hemmleb, Larry A. Johnson and Eric R. Simonson, *Ghosts of Everest: The Authorized Story of the Search for Mallory and Irvine*, Macmillan, London, 1999.

Pages 73-76 – My comments on Scott, Amundsen and Shackleton draw heavily on Roland Huntford's careful studies, *The Last Place on Earth* (1979; 2nd ed., 1999), and *Shackleton* (1985). On the *Endurance* expedition see also Frank Worsley, *The Great Antarctic Rescue: Shackleton's Boat Journey*, W. W. Norton, London, 1977, and Caroline Alexander, *The Endurance: Shackleton's Legendary Antarctic Expedition*, Bloomsbury, London, 1998. Alexander's book contains many previously unpublished photographs of the expedition by Frank Hurley.

Pages 96-97 – Lao Tzu (legendary), *Tao Te Ching* (compiled c. mid 3rd century BC), trans. D. C. Lau, Penguin, Harmondsworth, Chs. 37, 57, 63.

Chapter 9
Page 107 – According to tradition, the great Sufi poet Rumi (1207–1273) composed his formally perfect poems while in a mystical trance. This translation is from Coleman Barks, with John Moyne, A. J. Arberry and Reynold Nicholson, *The Essential Rumi*, HarperSanFrancisco, San Francisco, 1995.

Chapter 10
Page 125 – On Mt Hua, see AV, 'Cultural Strata of Hua Shan, The Holy Peak of the West, *Monumenta Serica*, vol. 39, 1990–91, 1–30. On Ou–yang Hsiu (1002–72), see James Liu, *Ou–Yang Hsiu: An Eleventh Century Neo–Confucianist*, Stanford U. P., Stanford CA., 1967; Ronald Egan, *The Literary Works of Ou–yang Hsiu*, Cambridge U. P., New York, 1984; J. P. Seaton, *Love and Time: Poems of Ou–yang Hsiu*, Copper Canyon Press, Port Townsend, 1989.

Chapter 11
Pages 135-48 – The main source on Douglas is John Pascoe, *Mr Explorer Douglas*, revised by Graham Langton, Canterbury University Press, Christchurch, 2000. I have also drawn on A. P. Harper, *Pioneer Work in the Alps of New Zealand*, and *Memories of Mountains and Men*, Simpson and Williams, Christchurch, 1946; Bob McKerrow, 'Charlie Douglas: His Final Years', *New Zealand Alpine Journal*, 1995, 99–100; M. V. Mueller, ed., *My Dear Bannie: Gerhard Mueller's Letters From the West Coast 1865–66*, Pegasus Press, Christchurch, 1958.

Pages 136-37 – Aristophanes (c. 445–386 BC), *The Frogs*, trans. David Barrett, Penguin, Harmondsworth, 1964.

Page 143 – Pindar (518–? BC), Pythian Ode 2, *The Odes of Pindar*, trans. Richmond Lattimore, University of Chicago Press, Chicago, 1947, 51.

Pages 143-44 – Haast's son gives a frank description of his father's method in *The Life and Times of Sir Julius von Haast*, 247, also 212–13, 253–54.

Page 146 – Baldesar Castiglione (1479–1529), *The Book of the Courtier*, trans. Charles S. Singleton, Doubleday, New York, 1959, Pt. 1 Ch. 6.

Pages 146-47 – Meng Chih Fan is mentioned by Confucius (551–479 BC), *The Analects*, trans. D. C. Lau, Penguin, Harmondsworth, 1979, VI, 15.

Chapter 12

Page 149 – Ssu–ma Ch'ien (c. 145– c. 87 BC), China's greatest historian, wrote his Letter to Jen Shao–ch'ing to explain, amongst other things, why he had chosen to submit to the degrading punishment of castration, rather than taking the 'honourable' path of suicide, after having angered the Emperor by speaking out in defence of a defeated general. His letter contains one of the most famous statements on friendship in Chinese literature: 'As the saying goes, "For who do you do it? Who will you get to listen to you?" Why did Po–ya never play his zither again after Chung Tzu–ch'i died? A noble man acts for a friend who understands him, just as a women makes herself attractive for her lover.' Unfortunately the gender aspect of the last sentence grates a little on modern ears. Po–ya was an outstanding musician who is said, on the death of his friend Chung Tzu–ch'i, to have destroyed his instrument because there was no longer anyone able to appreciate his playing. The complete letter is translated by J. R. Hightower, in Cyril Birch, ed., *Anthology of Chinese Literature*, Grove press, New York, 1965.

ABOUT THE AUTHOR

Aat Vervoorn was born in The Netherlands and grew up in Australia and New Zealand. During the 1960s and 1970s he worked as a mountain guide and instructor in the Mt Cook/Westland section of New Zealand's Southern Alps, and has continued to make regular climbing trips to this area. He is the head of the Centre for Asian Societies and Histories at the Australian National University in Canberra, where he lives with his wife Janette and two daughters, Cornelia and Saskia. His previous publications include *Beyond the Snowline*, *Men of the Cliffs and Caves: The Chinese Eremitic Tradition to the End of the Han Dynasty*, and *Re Orient: Change in Asian Societies*.